NIST Special Publication 800-95

Guide to Secure Web Services

Recommendations of the National Institute of Standards and Technology

Anoop Singhal
Theodore Winograd
Karen Scarfone

COMPUTER SECURITY

Computer Security Division
Information Technology Laboratory
National Institute of Standards and Technology
Gaithersburg, MD 20899-8930

August 2007

U.S. Department of Commerce

Carlos M. Gutierrez, Secretary

National Institute of Standards and Technology

William Jeffrey, Director

Reports on Computer Systems Technology

The Information Technology Laboratory (ITL) at the National Institute of Standards and Technology (NIST) promotes the U.S. economy and public welfare by providing technical leadership for the nation's measurement and standards infrastructure. ITL develops tests, test methods, reference data, proof of concept implementations, and technical analysis to advance the development and productive use of information technology. ITL's responsibilities include the development of technical, physical, administrative, and management standards and guidelines for the cost-effective security and privacy of sensitive unclassified information in Federal computer systems. This Special Publication 800-series reports on ITL's research, guidance, and outreach efforts in computer security and its collaborative activities with industry, government, and academic organizations.

National Institute of Standards and Technology Special Publication 800-95
Natl. Inst. Stand. Technol. Spec. Publ. 800-95, 128 pages (Aug. 2007)

Acknowledgements

The authors, Anoop Singhal and Karen Scarfone of the National Institute of Standards and Technology (NIST) and Theodore Winograd of Booz Allen Hamilton, wish to thank their colleagues who contributed technical content to this document, especially Holly Lynne McKinley, Patrick Holley, and Karen Mercedes Goertzel of Booz Allen Hamilton. The authors would like to acknowledge Tim Grance, David Ferraiolo, and Rick Kuhn of NIST, Jeremy Epstein of Web Methods and David Kleiner, Michael Colon, Steven Lavenhar, and Victoria Thompson of Booz Allen Hamilton, for their keen and insightful assistance throughout the development of the document.

Table of Contents

List of Appendices

List of Figures

List of Tables

Executive Summary

The advance of Web services technologies promises to have far-reaching effects on the Internet and enterprise networks. Web services based on the eXtensible Markup Language (XML), SOAP, and related open standards, and deployed in Service Oriented Architectures (SOA) allow data and applications to interact without human intervention through dynamic and ad hoc connections. Web services technology can be implemented in a wide variety of architectures, can co-exist with other technologies and software design approaches, and can be adopted in an evolutionary manner without requiring major transformations to legacy applications and databases.

The security challenges presented by the Web services approach are formidable and unavoidable. Many of the features that make Web services attractive, including greater accessibility of data, dynamic application-to-application connections, and relative autonomy (lack of human intervention) are at odds with traditional security models and controls. The primary purpose of this publication is to inform people about securing Web services. Difficult issues and unsolved problems exist, such as protecting the following:

- Confidentiality and integrity of data that is transmitted via Web services protocols in service-to-service transactions, including data that traverses intermediary services
- Functional integrity of the Web services that requires the establishment of trust between services on a transaction-by-transaction basis
- Availability in the face of denial of service attacks that exploit vulnerabilities unique to Web service technologies, especially targeting core services, such as discovery service, on which other services rely.

Perimeter-based network security technologies (e.g., firewalls) are inadequate to protect SOAs for the following reasons:

- SOAs are dynamic and can seldom be fully constrained to the physical boundaries of a single network.
- SOAP is transmitted over HyperText Transfer Protocol (HTTP), which is allowed to flow without restriction through most firewalls.

Moreover, Transport Layer Security (TLS), which is used to authenticate and encrypt Web-based messages, is inadequate for protecting SOAP messages because it is designed to operate between two endpoints. TLS cannot accommodate Web services' inherent ability to forward messages to multiple other Web services simultaneously.

The Web service processing model requires the ability to secure SOAP messages and XML documents as they are forwarded along potentially long and complex chains of consumer, provider, and intermediary services. The nature of Web services processing makes those services subject to unique attacks, as well as variations on familiar attacks targeting Web servers.

Ensuring the security of Web services involves augmenting traditional security mechanisms with security frameworks based on use of authentication, authorization, confidentiality, and integrity mechanisms. This document describes how to implement those security mechanisms in Web services. It also discusses how to make Web services and portal applications robust against the attacks to which they are subject. The following is a summary of security techniques for Web services:

- **Confidentiality of Web service messages using XML Encryption[1].** This is a specification from the World Wide Web Consortium (W3C) and it provides a mechanism to encrypt XML documents.

- **Integrity of Web service messages using XML Signature[2].** This is a specification produced jointly by the W3C and the Internet Engineering Task Force (IETF). The power of XML Signature is to selectively sign XML data.

- **Web service authentication and authorization using XML Signature,** Security Assertion Markup Language (SAML) and eXtensible Access Control Markup Language (XACML) as proposed by the Organization for Advancement of Structured Information Standards (OASIS) group. SAML and XACML provide mechanisms for authentication and authorization in a Web services environment.

- **Web Services (WS)-Security[3].** This specification, produced by OASIS, defines a set of SOAP header extensions for end-to-end SOAP messaging security. It supports message integrity and confidentiality by allowing communicating partners to exchange signed encrypted messages in a Web services environment.

- **Security for Universal Description, Discovery and Integration (UDDI)[4].** Produced by OASIS, UDDI allows Web services to be easily located and subsequently invoked. Security for UDDI enables publishers, inquirers and subscribers to authenticate themselves and authorize the information published in the directory.

Challenges

While many of the Web services challenges have been met with existing standards, there are a number of challenges that standards organizations are addressing—particularly in the area of Web services discovery and reliability. The Web Services Interoperability Organization (WS-I) acknowledges that there are many challenges that have yet to be addressed. Some examples of these challenges are:

- Repudiation of transactions
- Secure issuance of credentials
- Exploitation of covert channels
- Compromised services
- Spread of malware, such as viruses and Trojan horses via SOAP messages
- Denial of service attacks
- Incorrect service implementations.

The following sections discuss several Web services security challenges in detail, including Web services discovery, quality of service and quality of protection, and protection from denial of service attacks.

Discovery

In Web services discovery, participants identify and compose Web Services Description Language (WSDL) specific services based on definitions in a UDDI registry. Due to the potentially large number of

---

1 *XML Encryption Syntax and Processing* is available at http://www.w3.org/TR/2002/REC-xmlenc-core-20021210/.
2 *XML Signature Syntax and Processing* is available at http://www.w3.org/TR/xmldsig-core/.
3 *WS-Security v1.1* is available at http://www.oasis-open.org/specs/index.php#wssv1.1.
4 *UDDI v3.0.2* is available at http://www.oasis-open.org/specs/index.php#uddiv3.0.2.

service candidates in the registry, performance rankings for algorithms used to search, match and compose services can vary from case to case.

As the set of available Web services expands, advanced tools to help identify services that match a customer's functional and security requirements become increasingly important. It is important for service providers to describe their service capabilities and service requesters to describe their requirements in an unambiguous and semantic way. Techniques that take advantage of Semantic Web technologies can improve discovery capabilities. The Ontology Web Language for Services (OWL-S) is an example, but more work needs to be done to integrate such technologies into Web service registries. In OWL-S, the service requester can describe the service requirements using terms from a semantic model. Reasoning techniques are then used to find the semantic similarity between the service description and the request to find a set of matching services automatically. While both UDDI and OWL-S can be used to specify the security properties of a Web service, such support is not inherent in the discovery system. However, W3C's Semantic Annotations for WSDL is a step in the direction of merging Web services discovery technology with semantic Web technology. Even with semantic Web services discovery, true automation will require that the requester be able to determine explicitly the security requirements of the provider in addition to its functionality.

End to End Quality of Service and Protection

Most Web services deployed do not provide guarantees for Quality of Service (QoS) or Quality of Protection (QoP) under the scenario of attacks. QoS is important in defining the expected level of performance a particular Web service will have. By prioritizing traffic, overall performance of the system can be improved. The WS-Reliability and WS-ReliableMessaging standards provide some level of QoS. Both standards support guaranteed message delivery and message ordering. The standard considers other QoS parameters, such as rate of failure or average latency, as out of scope because they are usually dealt with by lower layer protocols. For Web services to truly support QoS, existing QoS support must be extended so that the packets corresponding to individual Web service messages can be routed accordingly to achieve predictable performance.

Overlap between OASIS and W3C Standards

Similar and overlapping Web services security standards that are being developed by multiple standard bodies are a source of confusion to system developers. Moreover, these standards are constantly being updated, resulting in interoperability problems. There is a need for more formal specification and testing of standards.

Methodologies for Web Services Security

The main emphasis of Web services security today is on basic infrastructure (e.g., protocols and languages). As technology matures and Web services become widely adopted, there will be a need for methodologies and recommended practices for security to help developers identify assets to be protected, analyze possible attacks, and decide protection levels and tradeoffs.

Availability and Protection from Denial of Service Attacks

Availability enables a Web services application to detect a Denial of Service (DoS) attack, to continue operation as long as possible, and then to gracefully recover and resume operations after a DoS attack. There is a need for techniques to replicate data and services to ensure continuity of operations in the event of a fault. There is also a need for management and monitoring solutions to provide service performance and availability monitoring to meet certain service level objectives.

Security Actions to Consider

The items below are possible actions that organizations should consider; some of the items may not apply to all organizations. In particular, it is necessary to balance these actions against budget requirements and the potential risks an organization's Web services may face.[5]

- **Replicate Data and Services to Improve Availability.** Since Web services are susceptible to DoS attacks, it is important to replicate data and applications in a robust manner. Replication and redundancy can ensure access to critical data in the event of a fault. It will also enable the system to react in a coordinated way to deal with disruptions.

- **Use Logging of Transactions to Improve Non-repudiation and Accountability.** Non-repudiation and accountability require logging mechanisms involved in the entire Web service transaction. As of early 2007, there are few implemented logging standards that can be used across an entire SOA. In particular, the level of logging provided by various UDDI registries, identity providers, and individual Web services varies greatly. Where the provided information is not sufficient to maintain accountability and non-repudiation, it may be necessary to introduce additional software or services into the SOA to support these security requirements.

- **Use Threat Modeling and Secure Software Design Techniques to Protect from Attacks.** The objective of secure software design techniques is to ensure that the design and implementation of Web services software does not contain defects that can be exploited. Threat modeling and risk analysis techniques should be used to protect the Web services application from attacks. Used effectively, threat modeling can find security strengths and weaknesses, discover vulnerabilities and provide feedback into the security life cycle of the application. Software security testing should include security-oriented code reviews and penetration testing. By using threat modeling and secure software design techniques, Web services can be implemented to withstand a variety of attacks.

- **Use Performance Analysis and Simulation Techniques for End to End Quality of Service and Quality of Protection.** Queuing networks and simulation techniques have long played critical roles in designing, developing and managing complex information systems. Similar techniques can be used for quality assured and highly available Web services. In addition to QoS of a single service, end-to-end QoS is critical for most composite services. For example, enterprise systems with several business partners must complete business processes in a timely manner to meet real time market conditions. The dynamic and compositional nature of Web services makes end-to-end QoS management a major challenge for service-oriented distributed systems.

- **Digitally Sign UDDI Entries to Verify the Author of Registered Entries.** UDDI registries openly provide details about the purpose of a Web service as well as how to access it. Web services use UDDI registries to discover and dynamically bind to Web services at run time. Should an attacker compromise a UDDI entry, it would be possible for requesters to bind to a malicious provider. Therefore, it is important to digitally sign UDDI entries so as to verify the publisher of these entries.

- **Enhance Existing Security Mechanisms and Infrastructure.** Web services rely on many existing Internet protocols and often coexist with other network applications on an organization's network. As such, many Web service security standards, tools, and techniques require that traditional security mechanisms, such as firewalls, intrusion detection systems (IDS), and secured operating systems, are in effect before implementation or deployment of Web services applications.

---

5 For more information on risk assessment, see NIST Special Publication 800-30, *Risk Management Guide for Information Technology Systems* (http://csrc.nist.gov/publications/nistpubs/).

Conclusions

Web services are important drivers for the software industry. The primary goal of service-oriented computing is to make a collection of software services accessible via standardized protocols whose functionality can be automatically discovered and integrated into applications. While several standards bodies (such as W3C and OASIS) are laying the foundation for Web services, several research problems must be solved to make secure Web services a reality. Service description, automatic service discovery as well as QoS are some of the important problems that need to be solved.

Web services are increasingly becoming an integral part of organizational information technology (IT) infrastructures—even though there are still unmet security challenges. To this end, the development and deployment of secure Web services is essential to many organizations' IT infrastructures. However, Web service security standards do not provide all of the required properties to develop robust, secure, and reliable Web services. To adequately support the needs of the Web services based applications, effective risk management and appropriate deployment of alternate countermeasures are essential. Defense-in-depth through security engineering, secure software development, and risk management can provide much of the robustness and reliability required by these applications.

1. Introduction

1.1 Authority

The National Institute of Standards and Technology (NIST) developed this document in furtherance of its statutory responsibilities under the Federal Information Security Management Act (FISMA) of 2002, Public Law 107-347.

NIST is responsible for developing standards and guidelines, including minimum requirements, for providing adequate information security for all agency operations and assets; but such standards and guidelines shall not apply to national security systems. This guideline is consistent with the requirements of the Office of Management and Budget (OMB) Circular A-130, Section 8b(3), "Securing Agency Information Systems," as analyzed in A-130, Appendix IV: Analysis of Key Sections. Supplemental information is provided in A-130, Appendix III.

This guideline has been prepared for use by Federal agencies. It may be used by nongovernmental organizations on a voluntary basis and is not subject to copyright. Attribution is desired and requested.

Nothing in this document should be taken to contradict standards and guidelines made mandatory and binding on Federal agencies by the Secretary of Commerce under statutory authority, nor should these guidelines be interpreted as altering or superseding the existing authorities of the Secretary of Commerce, Director of the OMB, or any other Federal official.

1.2 Purpose and Scope

This publication seeks to assist organizations in understanding the challenges in integrating information security practices into SOA design and development based on Web services. This publication also provides practical, real-world guidance on current and emerging standards applicable to Web services, as well as background information on the most common security threats to SOAs based on Web services. This document presents information that is largely independent of particular hardware platforms, operating systems, and applications. Supplementary security mechanisms (i.e., perimeter security appliances) are considered outside the scope of this publication. Interfaces between Web services components and supplementary controls are noted as such throughout this document on a case-by-case basis.

1.3 Audience

The document, while technical in nature, provides the background information to help readers understand the topics that are discussed. The intended audience for this document includes the following:

- System and software architects and engineers trained in designing, implementing, testing, or evaluating Web services
- Software developers experienced in XML, C#, Visual Basic for .NET (VB.NET), C, or Java for Web services
- Security architects, engineers, analysts, and secure software developers/integrators
- Researchers who are furthering and extending service interfaces and conceptual designs.

This document assumes that readers have some minimal Web services expertise. Because of the constantly changing nature of Web services threats and vulnerabilities, readers are expected to take advantage of other resources (including those listed in this document) for more current and detailed information.

The practices recommended in this document are designed to help mitigate the risks associated with Web services. They build on and assume the implementation of practices described in other NIST guidelines listed in Appendix F.

1.4 Document Structure

The remainder of this document is organized into five major sections. Section 2 provides background to Web services and portals and their relationship to security. Section 3 discusses the many relevant Web service security functions and related technology. Section 4 discusses Web portals, the human user's entry point into the SOA based on Web services. Section 5 discusses the challenges associated with secure Web service-enabling of legacy applications. Finally, Section 6 discusses secure implementation tools and technologies.

The document also contains several appendices. Appendix A offers discussion of several attacks commonly leveraged against Web services and SOAs. Appendix B provides an overview of Electronic Business eXtensible Markup Language (ebXML), a Web services protocol suite developed by the United Nations Centre for Trade Facilitation and Electronic Business (UN/CEFACT). Appendices C and D contain a glossary and acronym list, respectively. Appendices E and F list print resources and online tools and resources that may be useful references for gaining a better understanding of Web services and SOAs, security concepts and methodologies, and the general relationship between them.

2. Background to Web Services and Their Relationship to Security

Organizations are adopting SOA to support their mission critical applications. SOA is a computing paradigm emphasizing dynamic service discovery, composition, and interoperability. Web services are a technology that can be used to implement SOA and are increasingly becoming the SOA implementation of choice.[6] For a SOA to truly meet its goals, applications must be secure and reliable. A large number of security standards have been proposed for Web services by a number of different organizations. This section provides an overview of Web services, the associated security challenges, and the standards available for securing Web services.

2.1 Introducing Web Services

There are various aspects of Web services: messaging, discovery, portals, roles, and coordination. This section uses an example Web service to illustrate the use of each aspect in developing a SOA application. The example consists of a loan processing Web service which relies on two other Web services: an interest rate service and a credit check service.

2.1.1 Web Service Discovery

To define the format of each SOAP message, W3C developed the WSDL. WSDL interfaces are created by each Web service and can be shared to allow dynamic binding. Through dynamic binding, Web services can communicate with newly added services without any additional programming or configuration changes. To facilitate the discovery of Web services, a discovery standard called UDDI was developed. UDDI allows Web services to search for one another dynamically. When combined with WSDL, Web services can easily discover and use new services at run-time without human intervention.

In the bank loan example, the loan service needs to discover the rate service before using it. The rate Web service is listed in the UDDI registry as a Web service capable of providing information about the bank's rates. When the loan service is initiated, the UDDI registry is accessed and searched for a Web service capable of providing the bank's rate information. The UDDI registry returned the rate service's Uniform Resource Identifier (URI) and details about how to access the rate service, which are derived from the WSDL interface. Figure 2-1 illustrates the discovery process.

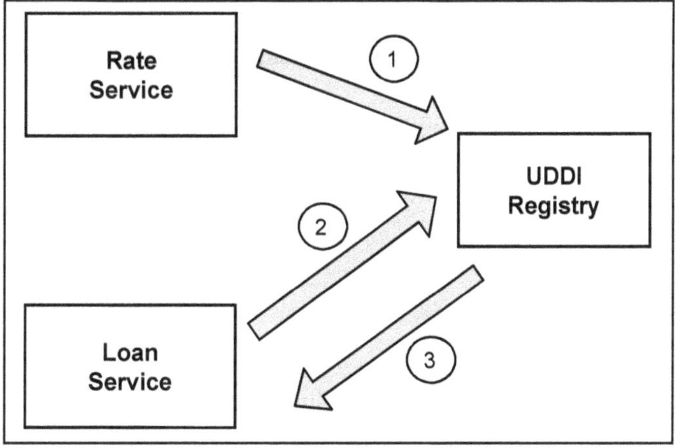

Figure 2-1. Web Service Discovery Example

6 A SOA can be implemented using a number of other technologies, such as Representational State Transfer (REST) or Common Object Request Broker Architecture (CORBA). This guidance is limited to SOAP-based Web Services, but much of the guidance in this document may be applicable to other SOA technologies.

1. The rate service's WSDL is mapped into a UDDI registry entry

2. The loan service queries the UDDI registry for a Web service capable of providing interest rate information

3. The loan service receives the rate service's entry and a URI to access the rate service

2.1.2 Web Service Messaging

Web service messages are sent across the network in an XML format defined by the W3C SOAP specification. In most Web services, there are two types of SOAP messages: requests and responses.[7] When a SOAP request is received, the Web service performs an action based on the request and returns a SOAP response. In many implementations, SOAP requests are similar to function calls with SOAP responses returning the results of the function call.

In the bank loan example, the loan service sends SOAP requests to both the credit and rate services to have them perform some calculations on data provided by the user. The loan service must have the credit check results of the individual to receive the loan and information about the current rates provided by the bank. Once both SOAP responses have been received, the loan service can determine whether or not to grant the loan to the user. Figure 2-2 illustrates how the loan Web service functions.[8]

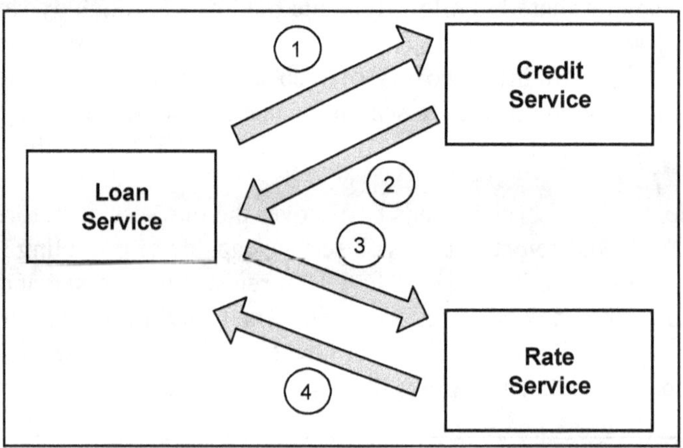

Figure 2-2. Web Service Messaging Example

1. The loan service sends a SOAP message to the credit service requesting a credit check be performed on the user.

2. The credit service sends a SOAP response back to the loan service with the results of the credit check.

3. The loan service sends a SOAP message to the rate service requesting a compilation of the current rates provided by the bank.

4. The rate service sends a SOAP response containing the current rates.

---

7 SOAP was designed to support many message exchange patterns (MEPs) in addition to request/response, such as one-way and peer-to-peer.

8 Figure 2-1 shows Web services communicating with each other serially. Services may communicate in parallel or asynchronously depending on the application or supported protocols.

2.1.3 Web Portals

A Web portal provides a human readable interface to the functionality provided by a Web service. Web portals are essential because many Web services are designed to be initiated on behalf of a user.[9] Figure 2-3 shows how messages pass between the user and the portal. When the user indicates that a particular action should be performed, the portal sends a SOAP request to the appropriate Web service, receives a SOAP response with the result of the action, and displays an appropriate response to the user. Web portals can provide access to more data sources than Web services alone, but almost all data sources can be implemented as Web services.

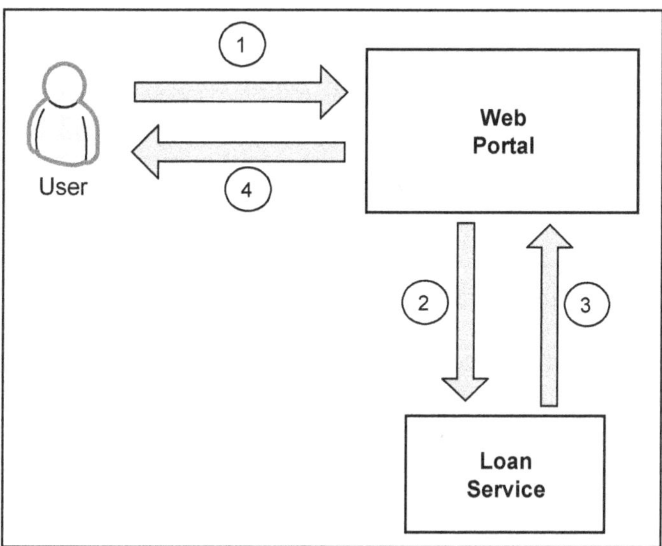

Figure 2-3. Example Portal Interface

In the bank loan example, shown in Figure 2-3, a user accesses a Web portal that gives the user the option of taking out a new loan. The user initiates the loan request, causing the Web portal to send a SOAP request to the loan service. Once the loan service completes its calculations, a SOAP response is sent back to the Web portal. The Web portal processes the SOAP response and generates an associated HyperText Markup Language (HTML) page for the user.

2.1.4 Web Service Roles, Modes, and Properties

The following sections summarize the overarching roles of the constituent components of a Web service-based SOA: requester, provider, and intermediary. These roles are not exclusive: a single Web service may be designed to act as a requester, provider, and intermediary depending on the context of the Web service transaction.

2.1.4.1 Requester Web Services

The requester initiates a Web service transaction on its own or on behalf of a user via a portal. The requester service is tasked with ensuring messages are in the proper syntax and taking the security measures required by the provider.

In the loan Web service example, when a user accesses the bank's Web site and makes a request for a loan, the loan service acts as a requester service and sends requests to the rate service and credit service.

[9] Other Web services may be initiated as part of a business-to-business (B2B) transaction or an application action.

After receiving the user's credit rating and the current rates, the loan service can then provide the user with a loan or deny the user's request.

2.1.4.2 Provider Web Services

The provider accepts a request from the requester and provides a response based on the input. The provider is responsible for setting the standards for authentication, authorization, encryption, and non-repudiation. The provider communicates its requirements through the extensibility of WSDL, a discovery service, or both. Some requirements may be negotiable, allowing requesters and providers to dynamically determine how to proceed, but at this time WSDL and discovery services do not provide a standard way for negotiating such requirements. Standards are under development to address this shortcoming.

In the loan service example, both the rate service and credit service are providers. When the rate provider receives a request, it performs the necessary calculations to determine the current rates offered by the bank. Once the request has been processed, the provider sends an appropriate response containing the bank's current rate information. When the credit provider receives a request, it returns a response containing the creditworthiness of the customer.

Web services provide a SOA in which applications are *loosely coupled*, allowing Web services to dynamically bind to other Web services at run-time depending on the needs of the user or application. Web services publish their functions to the UDDI registry so that other Web services can find needed functionality. This enables the reuse of applications, particularly legacy applications; by developing a Web services interface that is accessible via SOA, organizations can conserve resources used for costly migrations between platforms. Often, this results in a chain of Web service invocations and an associated performance penalty. This penalty, however, is often offset by the savings in development time and consistency of results associated with re-using components.[10] In a network with low latency and high availability, this performance penalty can be minimized to the point that it is not noticeable.

2.1.4.3 Intermediary Web Services

An intermediary service is a Web service that is invoked in a chain. The most common example of an intermediary Web service is an XML gateway that receives requests from requesters, performs security checks against the requests, and then forwards the requests to an internal Web service provider. From the perspective of the requester, there is only a single provider, but in reality there are two. There can be any number of intermediary services involved within a single Web service transaction. Figure 2-4 illustrates how multiple intermediary services may interact with other services.

---

10 While component re-use offers numerous benefits to developers, any implementation flaws in the component will affect all applications that rely on it.

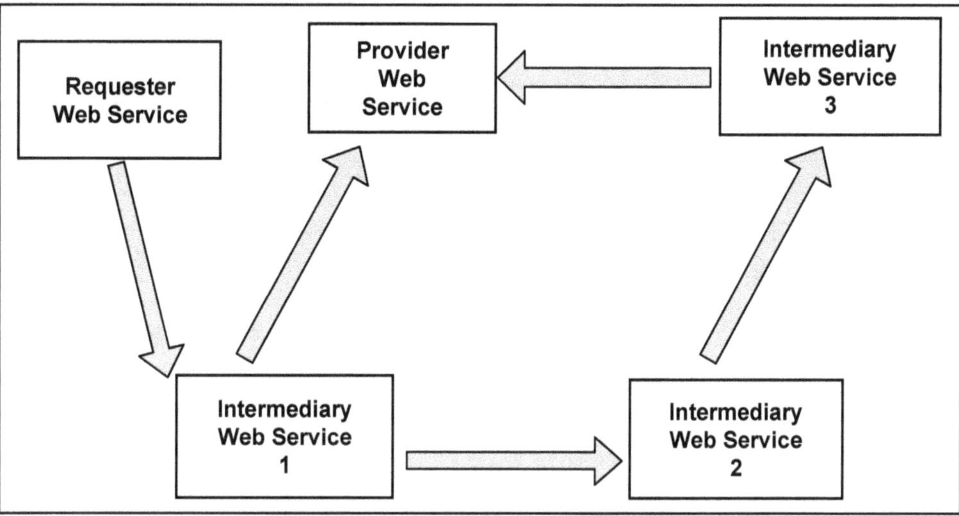

Figure 2-4. Intermediary Services

In the loan example, both the credit and rate services are intermediaries. As shown in Figure 2-5, the credit service receives a request from the loan service and then forwards the request on to the credit bureau services for each of the major credit bureaus. This allows the user's credit information to be checked by multiple sources while allowing the loan service to use a single service. As part of its calculations, the rate service may wish to make a request to a Web service that provides the current Treasury bonds rate.

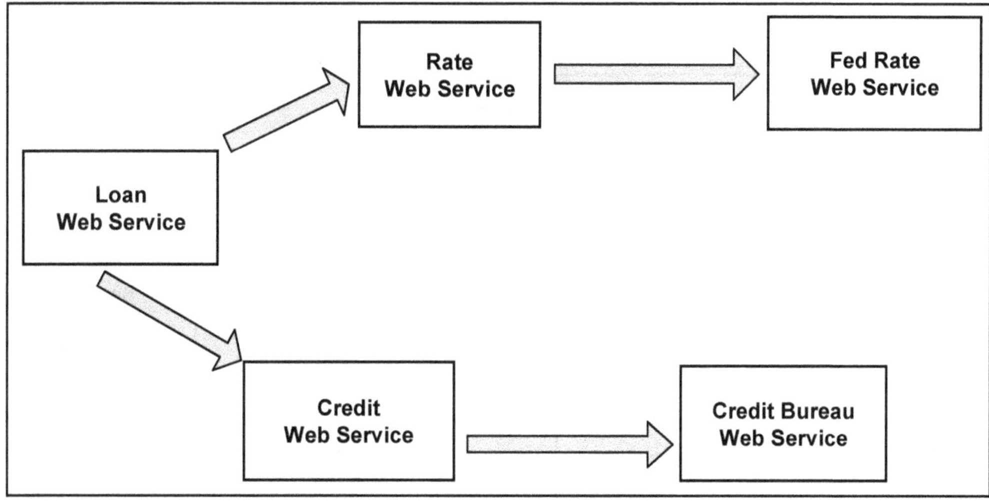

Figure 2-5. The Loan Service and Its Intermediaries

2.1.5 Coordination: Orchestration and Choreography

When multiple requesters, providers, and intermediaries are participating in a Web service transaction, it may be necessary to coordinate them. There are two different types of mechanisms for coordinating Web services: Web services orchestration and Web services choreography. Web services orchestration is performed within an organization's SOA and concerns the use of existing Web services to create another Web service. Web services choreography is performed among multiple organizations' SOAs and describes relationships between Web services so that Web services understand how to interact with one another to perform a process. Figure 2-6 illustrates how no single Web service is in control in a choreography.

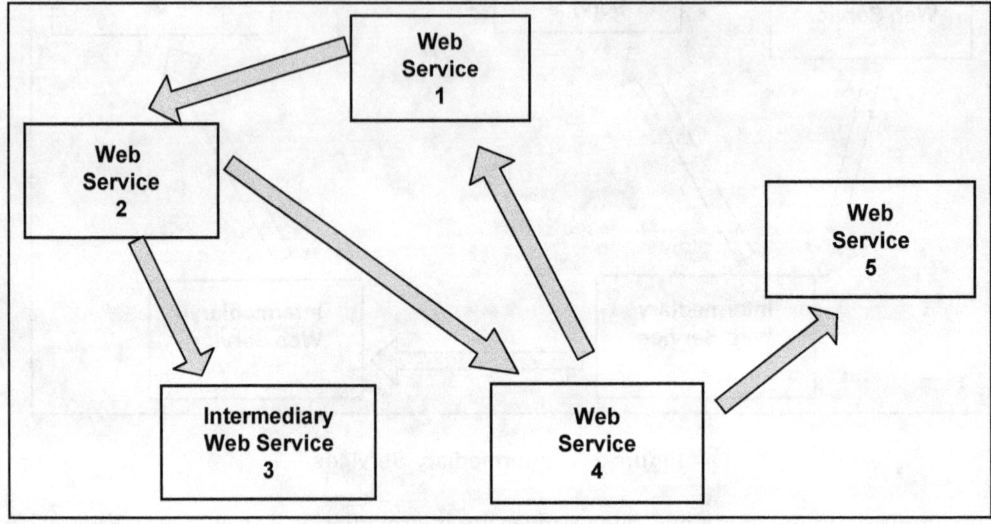

Figure 2-6. A Web Service Choreography

When invoking a Web service orchestration, the encapsulating Web service uses an orchestration engine to define which Web services will be invoked. In contrast, when invoking a Web service choreography, the sequence of Web services is more dynamic, and the decisions are made by the relationships defined between individual Web services rather than by a unifying orchestration engine. Figure 2-7 illustrates how the Web service orchestration is controlled by a single Web service.

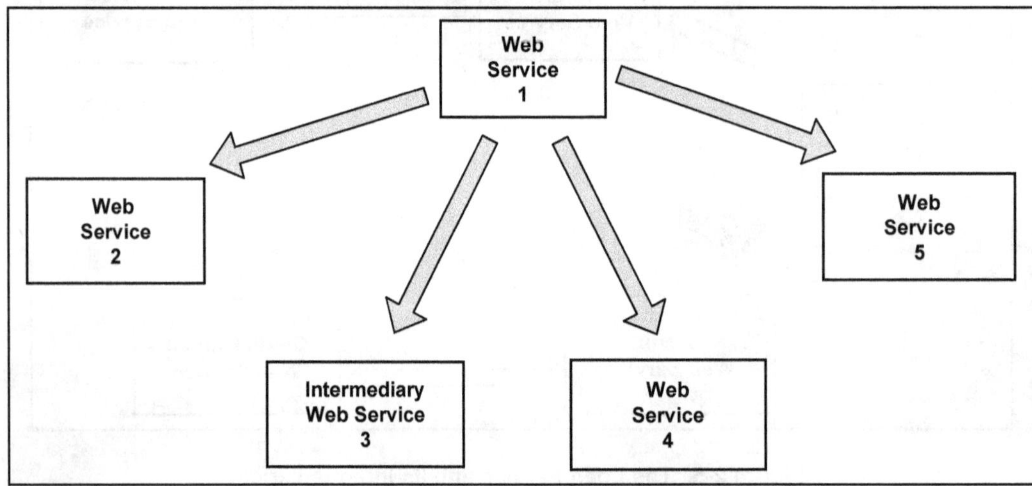

Figure 2-7. A Web Service Orchestration

Using the loan service example, the credit service could be implemented as a choreography. Each Web service in the transaction is not necessarily operated by the same organization as the credit service. Each Web service, the credit service and the individual credit bureau service, would enumerate the rules and expectations for interacting with one another. The credit service would dynamically look up the credit bureau service, process the information that is needed to interact with it, and then initiate a choreography among the services.

The rate service may be implemented as an orchestration, as all of the involved Web services would be internal to the rate service's organization. To fully calculate the interest rates that the loan service will use, the rate service consists of a chain of SOAP requests and responses passed from one internal Web service to another to gather the necessary information to respond with accurate rates. Each transaction within the orchestration is controlled by the rate service, so that requests and responses occur in the proper order and failures do not propagate throughout the transaction. Once complete, the rate service returns the result of the orchestration to the loan service, as shown in Figure 2-8.

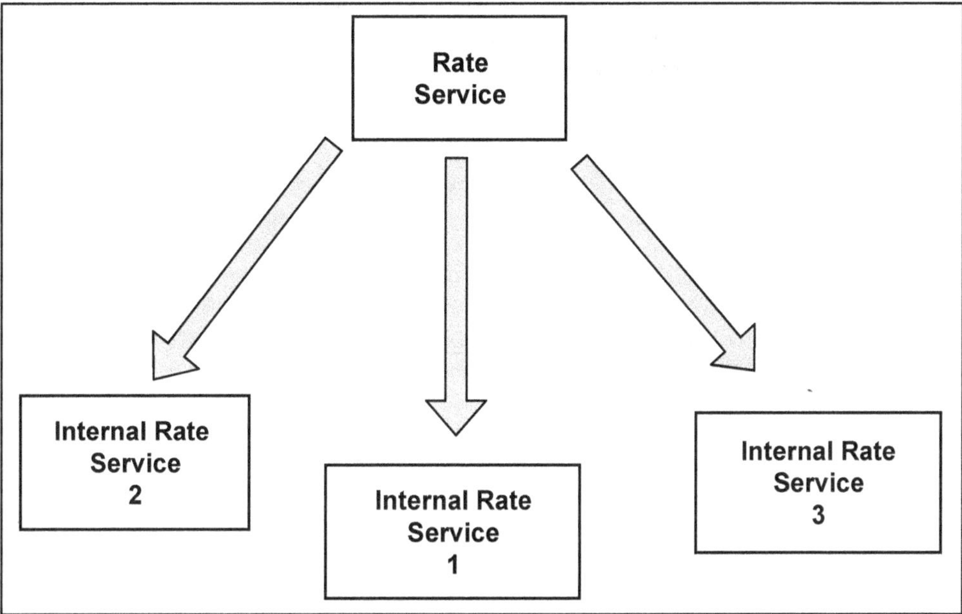

Figure 2-8. The Rate Service as an Orchestration

2.2 Elements of Security

Because a Web service relies on some of the same underlying HTTP and Web-based architecture as common Web applications, it is susceptible to similar threats and vulnerabilities. Web services security is based on several important concepts, including[11]:

- **Identification and Authentication:** Verifying the identity of a user, process, or device, often as a prerequisite to allowing access to resources in an information system.
- **Authorization.** The permission to use a computer resource, granted, directly or indirectly, by an application or system owner.
- **Integrity.** The property that data has not been altered in an unauthorized manner while in storage, during processing, or in transit.
- **Non-repudiation.** Assurance that the sender of information is provided with proof of delivery and the recipient is provided with proof of the sender's identity, so neither can later deny having processed the information.

---

[11] The definitions are taken from NIST IR 7298, *Glossary of Key Information Security Terms* and NIST SP 800-100, *Information Security Handbook: A Guide for Managers,* available at http://csrc.nist.gov/publications/nistpubs/. More information on these concepts can be found in *Computer Security: Art and Science* by Matt Bishop.

- **Confidentiality.** Preserving authorized restrictions on information access and disclosure, including means for protecting personal privacy and proprietary information
- **Privacy.** Restricting access to subscriber or relying party information in accordance with Federal law and organization policy

2.3 Web Services Security Dimensions

The Web services security dimensions have been defined as: secure messaging, resource protection, negotiation of contracts, trust management, and security properties[12]. These dimensions encompass the elements of security (discussed in Section 2.2) in a Web services environment. Each dimension is essential to the development of secure applications using Web services, but each dimension affects a different layer of the Web service. This section describes each security dimension and provides an overview of what technologies are available, what is on the horizon, and what remains to be done.

2.3.1 Secure Messaging

Web services rely on the Internet for communication. Because SOAP was not designed with security in mind,[13] SOAP messages can be viewed or modified by attackers as the messages traverse the Internet. There are several options available for securing Web service messages:

- **HTTP over SSL/TLS (HTTPS).** Because SOAP messages are transmitted using HTTP, it is trivial to modify a Web service to support HTTPS.
- **XML Encryption and XML Signature.** These XML security standards developed by W3C allow XML content to be signed and encrypted. Because all SOAP messages are written in XML, Web service developers can sign or encrypt any portion of the SOAP message using these standards, but there is no standard mechanism for informing recipients how these standards were applied to the message.
- **WS-Security.** WS-Security was developed to provide SOAP extensions that define mechanisms for using XML Encryption and XML Signature to secure SOAP messages.

Each secure messaging option has its own strengths and weaknesses. They are discussed in more depth in Section 3.6.

2.3.2 Protecting Resources

When resources are made publicly available, it is important to ensure that they are adequately protected. Usually, Web services are intended to be accessible only to authorized requesters, requiring mechanisms for access control. To perform access control, Web services need to identify and authenticate one another. Several different methods are available, including transport layer authentication, token authentication via the WS-Security specification using SAML assertions or other tokens, and the SOAP authentication header. Authorizations for Web services are often done through custom implementations, but the XACML is an OASIS standard available for performing authorization decisions, eliminating the time and cost associated with developing and testing a custom solution.

---

12 These dimensions are based on those defined in the paper *Securing Service-Based Interactions: Issues and Directions* by Hamid Nezhad, *et al* and can be found at http://dsonline.computer.org/WAS.

13 According to the SOAP specification, secure messaging was intended to be developed as an extension to the SOAP standard.

In the loan service example, the rate service is a provider service. When the rate provider receives a request, it needs to validate the identity of the requester and the supplied input. By validating the requester's identity, the rate service can check with organizational policies to determine whether the requester is authorized to access rate information. By validating the input, the rate service can ensure that the request includes valid and acceptable parameters. If the requester submits unexpected content, it is reason to suspect that an attacker may be probing the Web service for vulnerabilities. Once the request has been processed, the provider sends an appropriate response containing the bank's current rate information.

The challenges faced in protecting resources go beyond simply providing access control mechanisms. The goal of an attacker may not be simply accessing the Web service. Rather, the attacker's objectives may include disrupting the service, acting as a man-in-the-middle, eavesdropping on the service, impersonating the service, or even using weaknesses in the service's implementation to control the host platform. Typical threats to Web services are discussed in more detail in Section 2.6.

2.3.3 Negotiation of Contracts

One of the primary goals of SOA is to facilitate the automation of business processes by allowing services to automatically discover one another and immediately take advantage of the functionality offered. To facilitate business transactions, Web services need to be able to create, enforce, and abide by contracts between organizations. For example, a credit service relies on another organization's Web services. A contract between the two organizations ensures that all Web services will operate as expected and that the information passed between organizations will be properly secured. In many situations, these contracts are negotiated and agreed upon by the organizations before implementation can begin. Ideally, Web services would be able to negotiate and agree upon such contracts electronically, immediately after discovery during runtime to take advantage of new functionality immediately. Negotiating such contracts electronically opens up a number of potential legal ramifications for the organizations involved. Therefore, in lieu of this ideal, many SOAs rely on an implicit contract offered by the WSDL interface of a Web service and expect it to operate as advertised.

The ebXML[14] suite of standards provides tools for negotiating business processes and contracts using Web services. However, ebXML was developed as a replacement for Electronic Data Interchange (EDI) and, as such, is often considered too complex to use for regular Web services. Because ebXML Web services rely on SOAP, portions of the ebXML standards may be individually adopted for small organizations. Usually, the WSDL interface or registry entry of an individual Web service can be considered an implicit contract between the services, but there are no standards that support the enforcement of implicit contracts. Research in the realm of Web service choreography will aid in enforcing implicit contracts.

Web services may have specific QoS or QoP requirements. For example, a credit service may require that certain information be encrypted and signed using WS-Security, while the requester service may require a guaranteed response through reliable messaging. The ebXML suite of standards provides support for security properties in contracts, but it does not fully support automatic security properties negotiation. The WS-Choreography standard provides some support for negotiating security requirements. A promising area of research is Semantic Web services. Using Semantic Web technologies, Web services can intelligently search for other Web services with specific properties, including security properties. In addition, the Semantic Web Services Architecture (SWSA)[15] developed by the Defense Advanced Research Projects Agency (DARPA) Agent Markup Language (DAML)

---

14 More information on ebXML can be found in Appendix B and at http://www.ebxml.org.

15 The SWSA requirements can be found at http://www.daml.org/services/swsa/swsa-requirements.html.

Program specifically addresses negotiating contracts among Semantic Web services and the associated architectural requirements:

- **Negotiation protocol.** Web services require a protocol for negotiating properties of the transaction. Research is underway to develop negotiation protocols using Semantic Web technologies.
- **Negotiation service.** To facilitate negotiation, a provider that allows other services to offload negotiation can serve as a core service within the SOA.
- **Mediation service.** Services involved in negotiation may need to have disputes over various properties of the service contract mediated by a trusted core service.
- **Auditing service.** The resulting contract between services will need to be stored for non-repudiation services by a trusted core service.
- **Negotiation-enabled Web service.** Individual Web services will be able to inform one another that they support negotiation through the discovery process.

While these architectural requirements are specific to SWSA, these functions can prove useful when developing any SOA capable of supporting negotiation.

2.3.4 Trust Relationships

Web services standards are inherently flexible and have allowed several architecture models to evolve: a brokered trust model, a pairwise trust model, a federated trust model, and a perimeter defense model. While these models use the term *trust*, they are limited to being able to trust the identity of the service. Being able to establish a Web service's identity does not mean that the service itself is inherently trustworthy. There is always the possibility that a Web service has entered an erroneous state or has been compromised.

In their 1996 paper, McKnight and Chervany defined trust as "the extent to which one believes (and feels confident in believing) that the other person is trustworthy in the situation."[16] Based on this definition, authenticating the identity of a Web service may not be sufficient when determining whether or not to trust a remote Web service. When trust relationships span multiple organizations, the requirements for individual Web services will vary. For this reason, regardless of whether the provider is a trusted entity in terms of its identity, the requester should not presume that it will not send erroneous or potentially malicious content in a response to the requester's request. Similarly, because providers listen (like a server) for requests from various requesters, they should not presume that erroneous or malicious content will not be sent in place of valid requests. Nevertheless, identifying and authenticating Web services is an essential step in establishing trust. Each trust model provides different benefits and drawbacks, allowing trust to be supported in a wide variety of environments. With this caveat on the definition of trust in a Web services environment, the remainder of this document uses the term trust when discussing authentication to maintain consistency with standards and research papers.

The pairwise trust model is the simplest of all trust architectures, but the least scalable. In the pairwise architecture, each Web service is provided—at configuration—the security information of all other Web services that will be interacted with so that those transactions and Web services can be trusted. This approach eliminates the need for developers to coordinate with other entities, but it creates an unscalable and non-uniform security architecture because adding a new Web service would require adding new

[16] McKnight and Chervany's paper, *The Meanings of Trust*, is available at http://misrc.umn.edu/wpaper/WorkingPapers/9604.pdf.

information to all existing services it could interact with. When the SOA becomes large and dynamic, adding a new service can become time and resource intensive.

In the brokered trust model, an independent third party acts as a trusted third party (TTP) for the Web service. The requester and provider interface with the third party for a variety of security services. Unlike the pairwise trust model, Web services using the brokered trust model need to be designed with the broker's interface in mind, so that identity information can be properly retrieved by the Web service. This approach eases the distribution of identity information between Web services; each Web service will only need to verify the identity of the trust broker rather than the identity of all Web services in the SOA.

A federated trust model allows Web services from different organizations to seamlessly interact with one another via various federation mechanisms. It builds upon both the brokered and pairwise trust models by allowing organizations to use their own central trust brokers while relying on pairwise trust or brokered trust between organizations. Each organization that wishes to federate must do so following complex business procedures and protocols, but the end result allows the Web services of each organization to interact with few or no changes to their original configuration.

Another commonly used Web service architecture is the perimeter defense strategy. Devices known as XML gateways are placed between providers and requesters. An XML gateway acts as a proxy for the Web service by performing the security-related functionality in its place. Although XML gateways are useful tools in an organization's security strategy, they are not a panacea. Should an attacker bypass the XML gateway, all internal Web services will be vulnerable to attack. Internal Web services must be designed, developed, and configured securely.

2.3.5 Requirements for Secure Software

All software, including Web services, needs to satisfy requirements for performance, cost, usability, and security. Examples of possible requirements for secure software are predictability, correctness, and availability.

2.4 Meeting the Requirements for Securing Web Services

Several organizations, including OASIS, W3C, the Liberty Alliance, and various members of industry have put together numerous security standards and techniques for securing Web services. For the most part, these standards and techniques all complement or extend one another, but there are some conflicting or competing standards. This section provides an overview of the various standards and how they can be used to meet security requirements and protect against threats to Web services. Section 3 discusses the most widely accepted standards, technologies, and techniques in detail.

2.4.1 Secure Web Service Standards Stack

The open standards communities that created Web services developed a number of security standards for Web services. Figure 2-9 illustrates a notional reference model for Web services security standards. This reference model maps the different standards to the different functional layers of a typical Web service implementation. These layers are modeled after the OSI Reference Model but are not intended to be interpreted as strictly hierarchical.

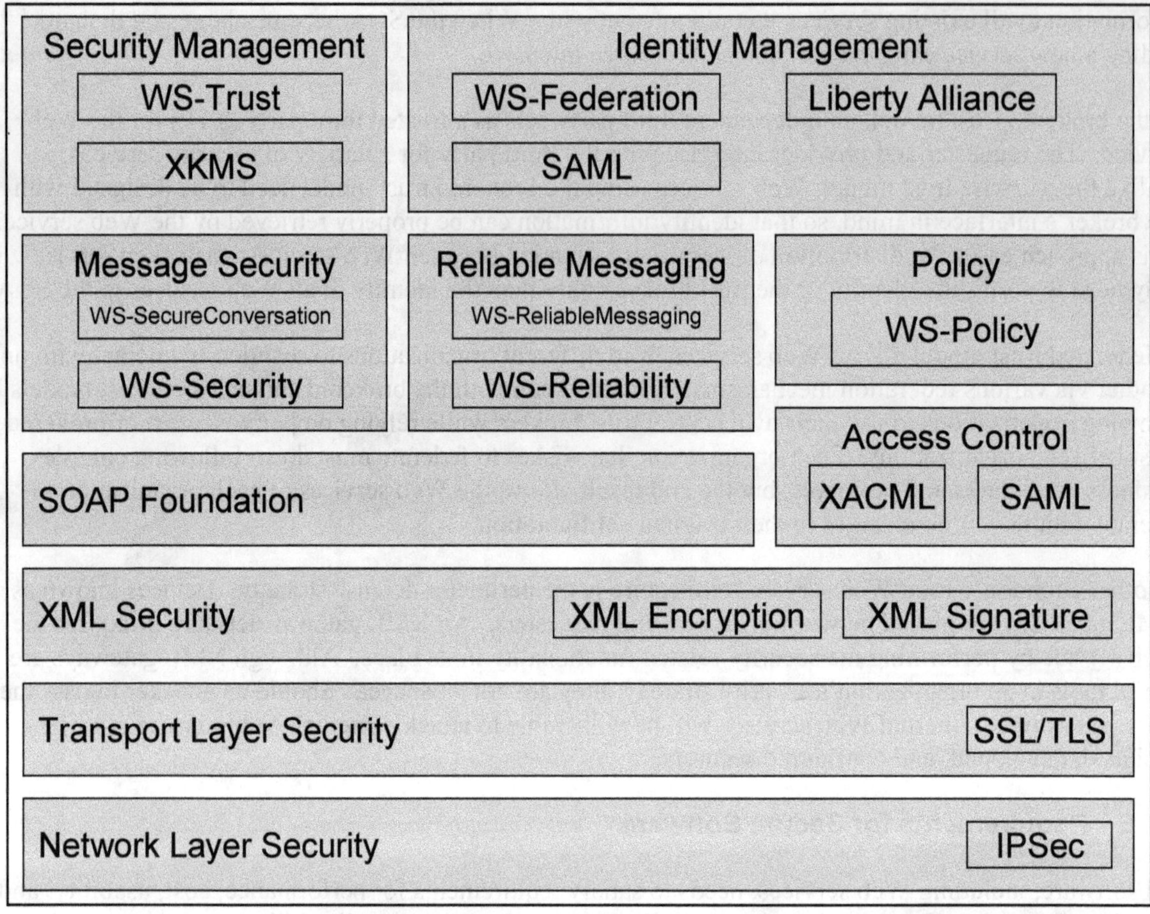

Figure 2-9. Web Services Security Standards: Notional Reference Model

Standards at the network, transport and XML security layers are used to secure messages as they are transmitted over the network. The security standards IPsec, SSL/TLS (Secure Sockets Layer/Transport Layer Security), XML Encryption and XML Signature each operate on SOAP messages at a different level.

Above the XML Security layer, there are two types of standards: standards built on top of SOAP and standalone standards. Message security standards WS-Security and WS-SecureConversation define how to use XML Signature, XML Encryption and credentials to secure SOAP at the message layer while reliable messaging standards define the protocols and constructs necessary to ensure that messages will be received. The access control standards are not unique to Web services; XACML can define the access policy for any system and SAML can be used to define assertions in any environment. The policy layer's WS-Policy defines a grammar to communicate the policy requirements of a Web service. These standards are described in more detail in Section 3.

Security management specifications define other Web services to manage credentials such as PKI certificates within the SOA. Identity management standards take advantage of access control standards, policy standards and SOAP standards to offer services for distributing and managing user identities and credentials within the SOA.

2.4.2 Relationship of Web Service Security Requirements to Standards

Table 2-1 shows which security requirements are satisfied by the various specifications and standards.

Table 2-1. Specifications and Standards Addressing Security of SOAs

Dimension	Requirement	Specifications
Messaging	Confidentiality and Integrity	WS-Security
		SSL/TLS
	Authentication	WS-Security Tokens
		SSL/TLS X.509 Certificates
Resource	Authorization	XACML
		XrML
		RBAC, ABAC
	Privacy	EPAL
		XACML
	Accountability	None
Negotiation	Registries	UDDI
		ebXML
	Semantic Discovery	SWSA
		OWL-S
	Business Contracts	ebXML
Trust	Establishment	WS-Trust
		XKMS
		X.509
	Trust Proxying	SAML
		WS-Trust
	Federation	WS-Federation
		Liberty IDFF
		Shibboleth
Security Properties	Policy	WS-Policy
	Security Policy	WS-SecurityPolicy
	Availability	WS-ReliableMessaging
		WS-Reliability

Each SOA security dimension has one or more security requirements. Each requirement may have any number of standards that support it. For example, both SSL/TLS and WS-Security provide confidentiality, integrity and authentication support for the messaging dimension, while the accountability requirement of the resource protection dimension does not have any supporting standards.

2.5 Core Services

The notion of *core services* has yet to be completely defined. Traditionally, these are services that can be used by any of the Web services in an organization's SOA. Two examples are the Open Grid Services Architecture (OGSA), developed for the Globus Grid, and the Department of Defense's (DoD's) Net-

Centric Enterprise Services (NCES), developed for the Global Information Grid. Both OGSA and NCES provide a set of services available throughout an organization that are commonly used or essential to most Web services, such as discovery, authentication, and authorization. OGSA provides a comprehensive list of what can be offered as core services: service management, service communication, policy services, and security services. Most SOAs use these same categories of core services but may provide differing names:

- **Service management services**: assist in managing a SOA by providing mechanisms to install, maintain, monitor, and troubleshoot Web services.
- **Service communication services**: provide support for various types of communications models between services: queued messaging, publish-subscribe event notification, and distributed logging services.
- **Policy services**: provide a framework for creating, administering, and managing policies for the infrastructure; these policies cover security, resource allocation, and performance.
- **Security services**: provide support for different security models, mechanisms, protocols, and technologies that extend core Web services security protocols to support activities such as authorization, authentication, trust policy enforcement, and credential transformation.[17]

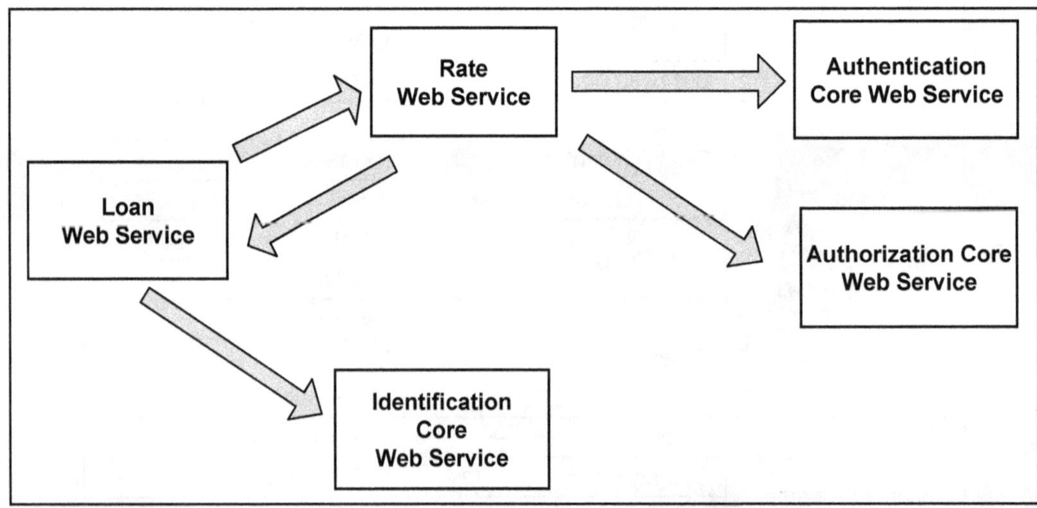

Figure 2-10. Core Services Used by the Loan Service

In the loan service example, shown in Figure 2-10, core services are used to offload identification, authentication, and authorization, among other capabilities, so that developers of the loan, rate, and credit services do not have to implement their own security functionality. For instance, when the loan service makes a request, it first retrieves an identifier from the identification service associated with the subject. When the rate service receives the request, it uses the authentication service to validate both the subject and the loan service. If authentication is successful, the rate service queries the authorization service to ensure the loan service and subject are authorized to receive policy information.

17 *A visual tour of Open Grid Services Architecture* can be found at http://www-128.ibm.com/developerworks/grid/library/gr-visual.

By offloading some of the processing to these core services, the implementation of the loan, rate and credit services is simplified when compared to a single Web service with similar functionality. This further improves security by lowering the number of possible defects that could exist in the individual services, but it introduces a slight performance penalty associated with the communication with the core services. Core services may also introduce a single point of failure in the SOA.

2.6 Threats Facing Web Services

Security decisions must always be made with an understanding of the threats facing the system to be secured. While there are a wealth of security standards and technologies available for securing Web services, they may not be adequate or necessary for a particular organization or an individual service. For that reason, it is important to understand the threats that face Web services so that organizations can determine which threats their Web services must be secured against. According to WS-I, the top threats facing Web services are:[18]

- **Message alteration.** An attacker inserts, removes or modifies information within a message to deceive the receiver
- **Loss of confidentiality.** Information within a message is disclosed to an unauthorized individual
- **Falsified messages.** Fictitious messages that an attacker intends the receiver to believe are sent from a valid sender
- **Man in the middle.** A third party sits between the sender and provider and forwards messages such that the two participants are unaware, allowing the attacker to view and modify all messages
- **Principal spoofing.** An attacker constructs and sends a message with credentials such that it appears to be from a different, authorized principal
- **Forged claims.** An attacker constructs a message with false credentials that appear valid to the receiver
- **Replay of message.** An attacker resends a previously sent message
- **Replay of message parts.** An attacker includes portions of one or more previously sent messages in a new message
- **Denial of service.** An attacker causes the system to expend resources disproportionately such that valid requests cannot be met.

The importance of these threats may vary depending on an organization's needs and purpose. In some instances, messages need not be kept confidential, so loss of confidentiality is not a concern. Similarly, organizations may offer a Web service to the public. For example, a Web service that provides information about the current weather forecast need not be concerned if a request is from a falsified sender. Regardless, it is important to understand these threats and what technologies are available to mitigate them.

The following Web services and HTTP standards can protect against many of these threats:

- **W3C XML Encryption.** Used by WS-Security to encrypt messages and provide confidentiality of part or all of a SOAP message

---

[18] More information about the threats and challenges facing Web services can be found in *Security Challenges, Threats and Countermeasures* at http://www.ws-i.org/Profiles/BasicSecurity/SecurityChallenges-1.0.pdf.

- **W3C XML Signature.** Used by WS-Security to digitally sign messages and provide message integrity and sender authentication
- **WS-Security Tokens.** Allows messages to include credentials to aid receivers in determining whether or not the message sender is authorized to perform the requested action. Supported token types include:
  - **Username/password.** The most common credentials in Web applications
  - **OASIS SAML Assertion.** Asserts that the sender has been authenticated and/or supply attributes associated with the sender
  - **IETF X.509 certificate.** Coupled with XML Signature, a receiver can verify that the CA issued the certificate used to sign the SOAP message
  - **ISO Rights Expression Language.** Used to provide public key information, attributes of those keys, as well as information about the sender's license
  - **IETF Kerberos token.** Allows Web services to exist in a Kerberos domain.
- **W3C WS-Addressing IDs.** Allows the message sender to supply a unique identifier for the message
- **IETF SSL/TLS.** Secures the HTTP protocol over which SOAP messages are sent and received
- **SSL/TLS with client authentication.** Requires both the sender and receiver to authenticate with one another before securing the HTTP protocol
- **IETF HTTP authentication.** Allows usernames, passwords (via HTTP Basic) or password digests (via HTTP Digest) to be sent as part of the HTTP header.

These technologies, along with other technologies that support them, are discussed in-depth in Section 3. Table 2-2 illustrates which standards provide protection against these threats. As the table shows, SSL/TLS and WS-Security, through XML Encryption and XML Signature, provide similar protections against threats; Section 3.6 discusses SSL/TLS, WS-Security and WS-SecureConversation and the trade-offs associated with each technology.

Table 2-2. Threats Addressed by Current Web Service Standards

	Message Alteration	Loss of Confidentiality	Falsified Message	Man in the Middle	Principal Spoofing	Forged Claims	Replay of Message Parts	Replay of Message	Denial of Service
XML Encryption		X		X	X	X	X		
XML Signature	X		X		X	X	X	X	
WS-Security Tokens			X		X	X			
WS-Addressing								X	
SSL/TLS	X	X	X*	X	X*	X*	X		
SSL/TLS with client certificates	X	X	X	X	X	X	X		
HTTP Authentication			X		X	X			

* Threat mitigated only for provider messages to requester, not for requester messages to provider.

As shown in Table 2-2, there are no standards that protect against DoS attacks. While the OASIS WS-Reliability standard and the work produced by the OASIS WS-RX technical committee address message reliability, ensuring the availability of Web services remains a hard problem. Many of the availability techniques used by high volume Web applications, such as load balancing, clustering and replication, can be used to aid in preserving availability.

Web services also face threats associated with all software: defects in a Web service implementation may lead to exploitable vulnerabilities. Web services, like Web applications, are remotely accessible, so attackers can take advantage of the Web service's availability to probe it for potential exploits. As with any remotely accessible service, it is important that Web services be implemented securely and that traditional network security tools and techniques be used to limit access to the Web service to only those networks and systems that should have legitimate access. Some aspects of secure Web service development are discussed in Section 6.

2.7 Common Risks Facing Web Services

As a software-based service that is network-enabled, Web services are at risk for many of the same security exploits that target any other software. An extensive listing and descriptions of common attacks targeting Web services appear in Appendix A.

Traditional security technologies are by and large inadequate to secure Web services. Perimeter-based network security technologies (e.g., firewalls, IDS) are inadequate because Web services are transmitted using HTTP, which is usually given free reign by firewalls, and SOAP may not be supported by an organization's IDS. While certain types of firewalls support filtering HTTP content, and some can support filtering SOAP, filtering all XML messages with traditional firewalls can prove to be expensive and reduce the throughput of the firewall. Due to the SOA paradigm, which allows for messages to be passed via intermediaries rather than simply by point-to-point communication, SSL/TLS is inadequate for a number of possible SOAP transactions because SSL/TLS is designed to secure transactions between individual Web services—and will not protect against an intermediary performing a man-in-the-middle attack. The SOAP specification explains that SOAP was designed with the intent of leaving security for an extension:

> "Two major design goals for SOAP are simplicity and extensibility. SOAP attempts to meet these goals by omitting, from the messaging framework, features that are often found in distributed systems. Such features include but are not limited to 'reliability', 'security', 'correlation', 'routing', and 'Message Exchange Patterns' (MEPs). While it is expected that many features will be defined, this specification provides specifics only for two MEPs. Other features are left to be defined as extensions by other specifications."[19]

WS-I has produced a document describing SOAP's security challenges, which include the following:

- SOAP does not perform any authentication between SOAP endpoints or intermediaries, so there is no way to verify the origin of a SOAP message.
- SOAP does not provide a mechanism for ensuring data integrity or confidentiality either at rest or during transit.
- SOAP does not provide a mechanism for detecting resubmitted SOAP messages.

The WSDL description of a Web service is usually automatically provided by the Web service framework used (e.g., appending ?wsdl to the Web service URI will return its WSDL) and may openly reveal the entire API of the Web service—even parts of the Web service that may have been disabled or that are used solely for debugging purposes.[20] Exposing too much information about a Web service through its WSDL descriptor may provide information about the design and security requirements of the Web service.

UDDI registries openly provide details about the purpose of a Web service as well as how to access it. In particular, UDDI provides tModels (described in Section 3.9.1) as "a way to mark a description with information that designates how it behaves, what conventions it follows, and what specifications or standards the service complies with."[21] Attackers may use this information to find potential flaws in the Web service. For example, the UDDI entry may show that the Web service uses a vulnerable specification. Any information in excess of that required to bind to the Web service may benefit an attacker.

Additionally, Web services use UDDI registries to discover and dynamically bind to Web services at run time. Because the UDDI specifications did not address digitally signing entries until version 3.0.2 (released as an OASIS standard in 2005), many UDDI registries do not provide a robust mechanism for verifying the authenticity of registry entries. This may allow malicious Web services to be added to the registry and used by other Web services.

---

19 *SOAP v1.2 Part 1 Messaging Framework* is available at http://www.w3.org/TR/soap/.
20 Any functionality intended for debugging purposes may be exploited by an attacker and should be disabled or removed.
21 UDDI v3.0.2 is available at http://www.oasis-open.org/committees/uddi-spec/doc/spec/v3/uddi-v3.0.2-20041019.htm.

2.8 Web Services' Interfaces with Network/Infrastructure Security Architectures

Because much of Web services security relies on XML Encryption and XML Signature or SSL/TLS, all of which use X.509 digital certificates to store cryptographic keys, most Web services frameworks seamlessly support and interface with a PKI. In particular, WS-Security supports the X.509 Certificate Token Profile. While the Web service itself does not need to implement XKMS or non-XML PKI protocols, PKI protocols should be supported by the host system to properly interact with the PKI.

In general, .NET and Java Web services rely on Windows and Java mechanisms, respectively, to store the various certificates that will be used by the Web service. By default, these key storage mechanisms require administrative interaction to fully interact with a PKI. Commercial off the shelf (COTS) products are available to integrate with a PKI. Additional Web services can also be developed to interact with the key management infrastructure.[22]

Web services frameworks provide support beyond simply abstracting the technical SOAP implementation. They often provide authentication and authorization services. Java Enterprise Edition (Java EE) and .NET both provide client authentication via SSL/TLS as well as sophisticated authorization services that can interface with any authentication mechanism. In particular, frameworks use widely used and robust libraries for authentication and authorization, which make these implementations less likely than others to have bugs. An additional security feature provided by Java and .NET frameworks is sandboxing, which is designed to separate all actions of the Web service from the operating system. Sandboxing affords added benefits to developers and administrators: stricter permissions and capabilities than those provided by the operating system can be applied to a Web service, and the sandbox helps to prevent the Web service from inadvertently or maliciously harming the underlying operating system, providing the sandbox itself is robust against attack.

Web services frameworks provide a number of benefits to developers in addition to well-tested tools and libraries: automatic creation of WSDL descriptors, client and server stubs, and potentially some implementation code. While this support can greatly improve the productivity of the development team, some developers may begin to rely on these tools when developing Web services and may not fully understand the code that is automatically generated. Should such developers be required to use a different development environment for Web services, they may not be adaptable and may inadvertently introduce security vulnerabilities. Additionally, the use of non-vetted, automatically generated code can itself lead to security vulnerabilities; most automatically generated code is intended merely to guide and aid developers, not for production use.

Developers need to be fully versed in the libraries supported by the framework when dealing with libraries that perform authentication, authorization, and other security functions that are not supported by the base framework. For example, XACML and SAML provide a flexible and platform-independent framework for distributed authorization. To properly implement XACML and SAML support may require overriding the framework's authentication mechanism at various points, which could lead to potential vulnerabilities in the Web service application. Supporting SAML or WS-Security in place of native authentication mechanisms may require the Web service to bypass authentication services provided by the framework, leading to potentially vulnerable code. Until frameworks provide native support for platform-independent authentication and authorization mechanisms, there will always be the potential for custom-developed code to be inadequately robust and lead to potential security breaches.

---

[22] More information on PKI is available in NIST SP 800-32, *Introduction to Public Key Technology and the Federal PKI Infrastructure*, available at http://csrc.nist.gov/publications/nistpubs/.

2.9 Summary

This section introduced the underlying concepts of Web services and the security challenges they face. The challenges have five dimensions:

- **Secure messaging.** Ensure that SOAP messages traversing networks are not viewed or modified by attackers. WS-Security and WS-SecureConversation provide the confidentiality and integrity services necessary.
- **Protection of resources.** Ensure that individual Web services are adequately protected through appropriate identification, authentication, and access control mechanisms. There is a plethora of standards available for controlling access to Web services.
- **Negotiation of contracts.** To truly meet the goals of SOA and automate business processes, Web services should be capable of negotiating business contracts as well as the QoP and QoS of the associated transactions. While this remains a hard problem, standards are emerging to address portions of contract negotiation—particularly in the QoP and QoS field.
- **Trust management.** One of the underlying principles of security is ensuring that all entities involved in a transaction trust one another. To this end, Web services support a variety of trust models that can be used to enable Web services to trust the identities of entities within the SOA.
- **Security properties.** All Web service security processes, tools, and techniques rely on secure implementation. A vulnerable Web service may allow attackers to bypass many—if not all—of the security mechanisms discussed in Section 3.

To adequately meet the challenges posed by each security dimension, the Web services community has developed a large number of standards. Each standard meets a different security challenge faced by Web services. WS-Security and SSL/TLS, for example, address the secure messaging domain, while WS-Federation and Liberty Identity Federation Framework (IDFF) address the trust management domain. Some security domains, such as messaging and trust management, are addressed by competing or overlapping standards, while others, such as the security properties domain, require further research within the community to fully address the challenges faced. Some standards address relevant security properties. For example, WS-Reliability and WS-ReliableMessaging provide some QoS functionality, allowing guaranteed message passing even if the network is under attack. More standards and technology are necessary to provide full support for all of the necessary security properties. When determining which Web services standards and technologies to adopt, it is important to be aware of the threats facing an organization's Web services and prioritize them to ensure that resources are distributed appropriately for the Web services being secured.

3. Web Service Security Functions and Related Technologies

Web service security standards, functions, and technologies continue to evolve at a rapid pace, driven by changes in the types of software attacks, community stakeholders, and Web services policy decision makers. This section describes several current and emerging standards, initiatives, and techniques aimed at improving the security of Web services. Many of the concepts used in securing Web applications are useful for understanding the security of Web services. Several resources on the subject of Web application security are provided in Appendix F for further reference.

3.1 Service-to-Service Authentication

Authentication is required to limit access to resources, to identify participants in transactions, and to create seamless personalization of information based on identity. A means of sharing the fact that authentication has been performed successfully is necessary to support single sign-on, allowing users to authenticate with one system and use other services and applications within a SOA.

Service-to-service authentication can be performed using a variety of methods, from HTTP-based token authentication to SSL/TLS-certificate based authentication, or by passing tokens along with the SOAP request. The HTTP and SSL/TLS-based methods are performed below the SOAP message layer and are transparent to the Web services involved, while SOAP-based token protocols require interaction between Web services.

Token-based Web services authentication is usually performed using the OASIS WS-Security standard, which supports tokens based on a variety of authentication standards: usernames, X.509 PKI certificates, Kerberos tickets, or SAML assertions (SAML is discussed in-depth in Section 3.5.3). WS-Security libraries are available for most of the widely used Java and .NET Web services development platforms. When a service provider attempts to access a remote Web service on behalf of a user, it should send an authentication token within a WS-Security message. These tokens convey that the initiating entity (e.g., a user or requester) has been authenticated and provide information about the entity, such as the authentication mechanism, time, and possibly subject attributes that may be applicable. Often, these tokens take the form of a SAML assertion.

For authenticating Web services between organizations using identity federation, the Liberty Alliance developed Liberty ID-WSF, which supports service-to-service authentication based on pairwise trust and federated identity. Federated authentication can also be performed using the WS-Trust and WS-Federation specifications developed to support WS-Security. Web service authentication using SAML and WS-Security is described in the following section. Identity federation technologies are discussed in-depth in Section 3.2.

3.1.1 Service Chaining

Sometimes, a service provider may not be able to perform the actions that a user or requester wishes it to perform, but it knows of a remote Web service that can. The service provider may invoke another remote service to satisfy the requester's request, which is known as *service chaining*. The service provider may use a SAML assertion, a WS-Security message, or both to make certain that both Web services trust each other.

There are two different approaches to service chaining. The Web service can access the remote Web service either as itself or by taking on the identity of the originator of the request. In the first case, the two Web services would communicate with each other as normal. In the second case, the remote Web service needs to be provided the identity of the originator in a trusted fashion. This can be satisfied using WS-Security and SAML.

There are two ways to pass the identity of the originator on to a remote service. First, if the Web service received a SAML assertion with the originator's request, that SAML assertion can be passed on to the remote Web service. It may be necessary for the requester service to sign either the SAML assertion or the SOAP message so that its own identity is passed to the remote service as well. Another option is for the requester service to generate and sign a SAML assertion for the originator itself and pass this SAML assertion on to the remote Web service. In this type of configuration it is not possible for the remote Web service to determine who originally requested the information. This limitation may be a hindrance in chain of trust deployments, as the chain is limited to the last requester.

By contrast, if the originator's SAML assertion is used or is signed, it is possible to trace the request back to the requesting entity. By forwarding a SAML assertion to the remote Web service, the requester service is able to assert the identity of the originator of the request. By either signing the SOAP message using WS-Security or the SAML assertion, the remote Web service is provided with the identity of the requester and can then determine whether or not it will trust the SAML assertion provided. If the authentication information requires confidentiality, SSL/TLS or WS-Security's encryption functionality should be used.

The use of signed SAML authentication or authorization assertions should be approached with caution. A signed SAML assertion is a token that can be reused by an attacker or a malicious service. Care must be taken to ensure that timestamps and validity periods are used and enforced. To address this, SAML assertions can be cryptographically bound to individual SOAP messages by signing the parent tag of the SAML assertion (e.g., using WS-Security to sign the Security element rather than the contained SAML token). While the SAML assertion may be reused, it will be invalid unless the entire signed portion of the message is also re-used, making it easier for service providers to detect replay attacks.

3.1.2 WS-Security for Authentication

Many Web services rely on the authentication mechanisms provided by HTTP and SSL/TLS. These solutions are only acceptable over a direct connection between two SOAP endpoints. If a SOAP message is to travel between multiple SOAP endpoints before reaching its destination, it is not acceptable to rely on HTTP and SSL/TLS for authentication, confidentiality, and integrity. There is no guarantee in this type of configuration that one of the Web services that handled the message did not misuse or store the data. In 2002, Microsoft, IBM, and Verisign released the WS-Security specification to address this shortcoming. In 2003, WS-Security was submitted as an OASIS standard, and in 2004 it was released as an OASIS standard. The ability of WS-Security to provide authentication (as well as confidentiality and integrity) at the SOAP message level is important for Web services to trust the messages they receive.

Authentication in WS-Security is performed by including *claims* in the WS-Security header of a SOAP message. Claims provide information about the identity of the SOAP message sender which can then be used to determine whether or not the sender is authorized to access the resources requested. Claims can either be endorsed or unendorsed. An endorsed claim, such as an X.509 certificate, provides inherent proof that the sender is the entity referenced, because the key referenced in the X.509 certificate can be used to verify the signed portion of the SOAP message. An example of an unendorsed claim is a username/password pair or a SAML assertion. In an unendorsed claim, there is no inherent method for determining that the sender of the SOAP message is the entity that the header specifies.

WS-Security also provides mechanisms for encrypting and signing elements of a SOAP message, including any WS-Security tokens. WS-Security explains how to use the XML Security and specifications within SOAP messages and what headers and elements are necessary to correctly process the ciphertext.

3.1.3 Security Concerns of WS-Security

There are several concerns prevalent in a WS-Security compliant Web service. Many of these concerns are not specific to WS-Security and apply to message integrity and confidentiality mechanisms in general.

WS-Security can be susceptible to replay attacks. An attacker may be able to reuse a WS-Security packet that is recorded. To mitigate this problem, timestamps, sequence numbers, and expirations should be sent signed within the WS-Security message. The receiving endpoint should then check to make sure that the message received has not been replayed.

WS-Security provides support for tokens that can be sent in the WS-Security header of a SOAP message. Without proper safeguards, these security tokens can be substituted. It is important when using WS-Security tokens to sign the appropriate portions of the message. WS-Security headers that are signed by the sender can be used to detect alterations.

Credential management may be a concern with WS-Security. PKI is most commonly deployed using X.509 certificates. PKI is used in e-commerce for performing SSL/TLS transactions over the World Wide Web. In many security architectures, user credentials are presented in the form of X.509 certificates. To this end, XML protocols and Web services security protocols have been developed to work with PKIs and X.509 in particular. XML Encryption can use a PKI for encrypting XML messages while XML Signature relies on a PKI for digitally signing XML content using algorithms similar to those defined in FIPS 186-2[23]. As such, Web services innately support working within a PKI. Management of X.509 certificates and other credentials may or may not be provided by the SOA. While SOAP-compliant services exist to interact with a PKI (e.g., XKMS), most installed PKIs use older non-XML-based protocols which require certificate management to take place out-of-band from XML-based communication.

Most WS-Security, SAML, and XML Security libraries do not perform full certificate validation by default. All certificate libraries will validate to make sure that the certificate was signed by a trusted Certificate Authority (CA). Most certificate libraries are not configured—and may not adequately support—checking the certificate against the CA's Certificate Revocation List (CRL) or the Online Certificate Status Protocol (OCSP), the two main standards for detecting whether or not a certificate has been revoked. To support the more advanced features of PKI certificate management, either additional libraries or appropriate versions of the Web services framework should be used. For example, newer versions of Java (1.5+) support OCSP, and Microsoft's Windows XP and Windows Server 2003 support OCSP for .NET-based Web services. For some applications, they may need to interact explicitly with the CRL or OCSP responder through some API to fully use PKI certificate management. Some PKI libraries, however, will perform CRL or OCSP checking automatically when validating digital signatures. The use of CRLs, OCSP, and PKI authentication is described in more detail in FIPS 196[24], NIST SP 800-32[25] and NIST SP 800-25[26].

---

23 FIPS 186-2, *Digital Signature Standard*, is available at http://csrc.nist.gov/publications/fips/.

24 FIPS 196, *Entity Authentication Using Public Key Cryptography*, is available at http://csrc.nist.gov/publications/fips/.

25 NIST SP 800-32, *Introduction to Public Key Technology and the Federal PKI Infrastructure*, is available at http://csrc.nist.gov/publications/nistpubs/.

26 NIST SP 800-25, *Federal Agency Use of Public Key Technology for Digital Signatures and Authentication*, is available at http://csrc.nist.gov/publications/nistpubs/.

Attribute management can also be a concern with WS-Security. With the availability of SAML, many Web services may use Attribute Based Access Control (ABAC), which allows users to be authorized based on their attributes rather than their roles or user IDs. Attributes can include a user's role, location, nationality, organization or clearance. Attribute management is important even without ABAC, as Web services may require information about various entities during the course of a Web service transaction.

3.2 Identity Management

Identity management for SOA encompasses the full range of identity-related events, information, and documents by which an entity's identity is verified, identity documents and credentials are issued to the entity, and entity identities are authenticated at point of entry into the SOA. In the SOA, an entity's identity forms the basis for both authorization and trust.

An Identity Management System (IDMS), such as that pictured in Figure 3-1, is responsible for verifying the identities of entities, registering them, and issuing them digital identifiers. In accordance with Homeland Security Presidential Directive (HSPD) 12, Subject: Policy for a Common Identification Standard for Federal Employees and Contractors[27], NIST Federal Information Processing Standard (FIPS) 201-1, *Personal Identity Verification of Federal Employees and Contractors*[28], describes a number of requirements that must be satisfied before a human entity may be registered in a Federal IDMS, including a National Agency Check and Inquiries (NACI) background check. Non-government organizations may have different rules for registration. For example, users who wish to gain access to many e-commerce sites often need to provide only a valid email address and a credit card number.

27 HSPD-12, *Policy for a Common Identification Standard for Federal Employees and Contractors*, is available at http://www.whitehouse.gov/news/releases/2004/08/20040827-8.html.

28 FIPS 201-1, *Personal Identity Verification of Federal Employees and Contractors*, is available at http://csrc.nist.gov/publications/fips/.

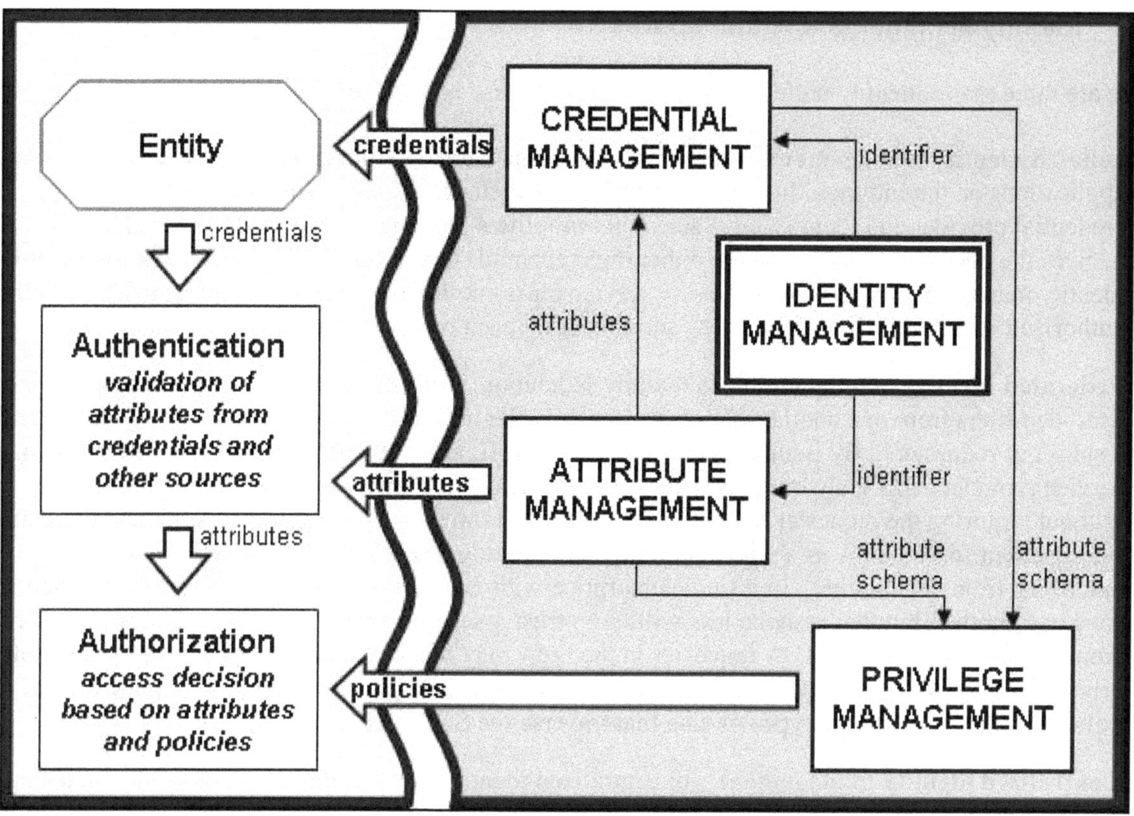

Figure 3-1. Identity Management Overview

Once an entity has been issued a digital identifier, that identifier can be used within that organization to associate other information with the entity, such as role and authorization attributes. The identifier may also become part of the digital credential that authorizes the entity to access different resources in the SOA.

Once registered, an entity must provide a portion of its credentials sufficient to authenticate that entity's identity. Again, different organizations have different policies for what constitutes sufficient authentication credentials. Many e-commerce sites require the entity to supply a username and password; other organizations may require the entity to submit an X.509 certificate.

After the entity's identity has been authenticated, the policy decision point (PDP) of the system or resource to which it desires access must determine whether the now-authenticated entity is also authorized to access the resource. To perform authorization, the PDP relies on privilege management and attribute management. Privilege management enforces the policies that govern entity access. The policy decision to allow or deny access may be based on a single entity attribute such as the entity's role, or it may require a combination of fine-grained attributes such as the physical location of the entity, its currently active role in the system, and its clearance level. The attribute management system uses the entity's digital identifier (issued by the IDMS) to locate and retrieve those of the entity's attributes that are required by the privilege management policy.

3.2.1 Identity Management Architectures

There are three major identity architectures[29] available for use in Web services:

- **Isolated identity management.** Isolated identity management is the architecture used by most Web applications on the Internet. In isolated identity management, service providers act both as a credential provider and identity provider. This simplifies management for a single service and negates the need for a TTP to handle either the credentials or providers. The drawback for an isolated identity management system is that every service must know the credentials and identifiers for all authorized requesters. In a large SOA, administering each provider may become unmanageable.
- **Federated identity management.** In identity federation, a group of providers agrees to recognize user identifiers from one another. Each service provider acts as a credential and identity provider for a subset of requesters. By issuing assertions (e.g., SAML authentication and attribute assertions), a service provider can supply other providers with the necessary information about the requester without requiring the requester to authenticate a second time. This simplifies identity and credential management for the SOA as a whole, but requires individual services to be aware of and trust assertions from one another. In a single enterprise-wide SOA, it may not be difficult for providers to trust one another, but they may be less willing to trust assertions when the SOA includes providers from different organizations. A requester in the SOA may make a request to a provider and supply an arbitrary assertion to gain access. In identity federation, it is important to develop organizational policies appropriate for the types of data that traverse the SOA.
- **Centralized identity management.** In centralized identity management, providers rely on a single TTP to provide credentials and identifiers to requesters. Centralized identity management is similar to federated identity management in that the identity and credential providers supply assertions directly to service providers, allowing requesters access without authenticating a second time. In this architecture, individual service providers need only be aware of the identity provider. In a cross-organizational SOA, organizations may be willing to trust another organization's identity providers more than individual services. A major drawback of the centralized identity management architecture is that the identity providers may act as a single point of failure. Should all of an organization's identity providers suffer a DoS, it will not be possible for providers to accept any requests.

When developing a new SOA or updating an existing SOA, it is important to consider the size of the SOA and the organization's priorities. One or more of these architectures may not be suitable for SOAs of a certain size or may violate organizational policies.

3.2.2 Laws of Identity

In May 2005, Kim Cameron, Identity and Access Architect at Microsoft, authored *The Laws of Identity*[30] based on his research into the requirements for a unified identity *metasystem*, a system of identity systems that exposes a unified interface for disparate underlying identity technologies. Organizations that follow these laws when developing or deploying an identity management architecture will be able to better support cross-organizational collaboration. The seven laws are as follows:

- **User Control and Consent.** Identity systems must not reveal identifying information without the user's consent.

---

[29] The concept of isolated, federated and centralized identity management architectures is drawn from "*Trust requirements in identity management*," available at http://portal.acm.org/citation.cfm?id=1082290.1082305.

[30] The complete text of Mr. Cameron's May 2005 white paper entitled *The Laws of Identity* is available at http://www.identityblog.com/stories/2004/12/09/thelaws.html.

- **Minimal Disclosure for a Constrained Use.** Identity systems must disclose the least amount of identifying information while simultaneously limiting its use as much as possible.
- **Justifiable Parties.** Identity systems must disclose identifying information only to parties having a justifiable need to know it.
- **Directed Identity.** An identity system must support both omni-directional and uni-directional identifiers. An omni-directional identifier can be shared with any third party while a uni-directional identifier can only be used between two parties.
- **Pluralism of Operators and Technologies.** An identity system must support multiple identity technologies and multiple identity providers.
- **Human Integration.** The identity system must define the human user as a component of the distributed system.
- **Consistent Experience Across Contexts.** The identity system must provide users with a consistent experience while enabling support for different technologies and providers.

Each of the major identity architectures discussed in Section 3.2.1 can be configured to follow these laws. By harnessing these laws, identity architectures can securely and adequately share identifying information amongst themselves so that large organizations or multiple organizations with differing policies and identity management architectures can better support a SOA.

3.2.3 Identity Management and Web Services

Web services provide a standardized mechanism for communicating and sharing information across organizational boundaries. To maintain accountability and ensure that only authorized users gain access to restricted operations or information, Web services must be able to communicate identifying information across these organizational boundaries. According to Axel Buecker and Heather Hinton[31], successful cross-organizational Web services require a way for providers to securely identify and provide services to authorized requesters and a way for requesters to securely invoke Web services with the necessary credentials.

Without an identity management framework, it becomes difficult for Web services to securely identify one another or provide recognizable credentials. For example, organization A may use X.509 certificates to identify Web services and individual users, while organization B may use Kerberos tickets for identification. If a requester from B sends a SOAP message with a Kerberos ticket to a provider from A, the provider will not be able to authorize the requester and will deny access. Identity management frameworks for Web services abstract this information and allow Web servers to securely identify one another regardless of the underlying identification technology. According to Buecker and Hinton, organizations need only develop a single set of Web services to facilitate Web service identity management across organizational boundaries:

- **Trust services.** These services issue and validate authentication tokens for use across boundaries. Trust services can also exchange these tokens with a local identity provider.
- **Authentication and validation services.** These services are provided by the local identity providers, granting tokens to authenticated users and validating tokens presented by a trust service.

---

31 The IBM Redbooks Paper, *Federated Identity Management and Secure Web Services,* is available at http://www.redbooks.ibm.com/redpapers/pdfs/redp3678.pdf.

- **Identity and attribute mapping services.** Often included within the trust services, these services map supplied identifying information or attributes to their local equivalents.
- **User lifecycle management services.** These services allow the establishment or mapping of identifying information and attributes for a user from a different organization.
- **Authorization services.** Often implemented locally for individual services, authorization services can process the credentials provided by the sender, query the appropriate security policy and determine whether the sender is allowed to perform the requested action.

Identity management systems may provide these abstract services in various configurations, with some being explicit Web services while others are implicitly supplied. Should an organization choose to implement its own identity management architecture, it should determine which of these services are necessary and implement them accordingly.

3.3 Establishing Trust between Services

For SAML or WS-Security to be useful on a large scale, trust relationships need to be established between remote Web services. A signed SAML assertion or WS-Security message is of no use if the receiver of the assertion cannot guarantee that the information asserted is trustworthy.

In the original SAML specification, only direct trust relationships are discussed—these are referred to as pairwise circles of trust. By contrast, SAML v2.0 provides two additional trust models for SAML: brokered trust and community trust.

Pairwise trust circles are the tightest and most direct form of trust relationship. Each entity that is authorized to communicate with another must share its key information. In a pairwise trust circle, if a SAML assertion can be verified, it is from an authorized entity. One major drawback of pairwise trust is that each entity must have a copy of the public key from every other entity with which it communicates, making the system inherently unscalable.

Brokered trust models are an extension of the pairwise trust model. When two services communicate that do not know each other's keys, a TTP is used to exchange the key information for them. This scales better than the pairwise trust circle because adding a new service provider involves simply exchanging its key information with the TTP. The Web service providers have to trust that the TTP has not been compromised. This differs from the pairwise model in which each service provider is independently responsible for trust.

Another difficulty with the brokered trust model is that there may be a situation where the two services can communicate with the TTP but should not communicate with each other. In the pairwise model, entities that should not communicate with one another would simply not have the appropriate cryptographic keys to do so, preventing any messages from being passed. In the brokered trust model, each entity can communicate with the TTP and thus with other entities. Either the TTP or the individual entities must know who should and should not communicate with one another.

The community trust model relies on an external PKI for establishing trust. This trust model assumes that the PKI interfaces are implemented correctly and that none of the certificate authorities have been compromised. This model provides simplicity similar to that of the pairwise trust model and scalability superior to the brokered trust model. If the remote entity's key can be retrieved through the PKI interface, a trusted authority has signed its key and it is safe to communicate with it. There must be a mechanism in place preventing two entities from communicating against policy even if they can retrieve each other's keys. This could be done either through PKI or the individual entities. Adding a new service is as simple as adding its key to the PKI.

Signed SAML assertions have the same security shortcomings as any technology that uses public key cryptography: the private key must not be compromised. The best way to protect against this situation is to keep keys secured and generate new keys on a regular basis. Once an attacker has compromised an entity's private key, that entity can be impersonated. [32]

Whether Web services need to trust one another within a single organization or across multiple organizational boundaries, trust federation frameworks provide support for all of the aforementioned trust models. Section 3.3.2 discusses the various frameworks available for federation of trust.

3.3.1 Federation of Trust

Trust in distributed computing environments is usually verified using PKI certificates signed by a certificate authority or by passing custom tokens generated by a TTP, as is done in a Kerberos environment. Traditionally, these trust mechanisms have worked well within a single organization. Once information sharing crosses organizational boundaries, entities communicating with one another do not necessarily have the same source of trust. Before the advent of Web services, information sharing across organizational boundaries traditionally was handled by using a proxy that bridges the boundary or by cross-signing certificates.

In a SOA, Web services from multiple organizations should be able trust one another without requiring extensive restructuring of the trust environment. To this end, trust federation frameworks can be configured to use an organization's pre-existing authentication mechanisms. Liberty Alliance provides both Web application and Web service federation using SAML to perform the trust brokering. WS-Federation allows different security realms to federate by defining trust brokers, who will validate security tokens used between Web services using WS-Trust.

The following subsections provide additional information on the trust frameworks identified above. It must be noted, however, that these frameworks continue to evolve. Thus, the material provided is meant to offer a current snapshot of the features they offer as of this guide's date of publication.

3.3.2 Trust Federation Frameworks

The following subsections provide additional details of the Liberty Alliance and WS-Trust frameworks. These standards provide similar features and functionality using different techniques and have been designed with different goals in mind. Determining which framework is best for a particular organization depends greatly on what is deployed and on the organization's architectural goals.

3.3.2.1 Liberty Alliance

The Liberty Alliance aims to develop a standards-based identity federation framework suitable for businesses and governments. Liberty Alliance-compliant products can interact with one another within a federated environment, allowing organizations to federate identities without having to agree on the same providers.

---

[32] More information on PKI is available in NIST SP 800-32, *Introduction to Public Key Technology and the Federal PKI Infrastructure*, available at http://csrc.nist.gov/publications/nistpubs/.

The Liberty Alliance has defined the Identity Web Services Framework, which defines how Web services can interact on a user's behalf through appropriate use of SAML by defining several services, including the following:

- **Discovery Services.** Allow Web services to dynamically look up the identity providers of a particular principal
- **Interaction Services.** Provide a mechanism for getting the principal's permission to perform various actions
- **Data Services.** Provide the Web service functionality that will be used on behalf of the principal
- **Identity Services.** Provide access to information about the principal that may not be provided by the SAML assertion associated with the Web service request.[33]

3.3.2.2 WS-Federation and WS-Trust

WS-Federation and WS-Trust were developed by IBM, Microsoft, RSA, Verisign, BEA, and several other vendors to create an identity federation system based on extensions to WS-Security that uses the core Web services protocols: SOAP and WSDL. WS-SecurityPolicy is an extension of the WS-Policy framework that allows a Web service to define a set of requirements detailing how messages should be secured and what tokens are required by the Web service. It is used by WS-Trust to determine what tokens are needed to interact with a particular Web service. As discussed in Section 3.1.2, these are referred to as claims.

WS-Trust is used to exchange trust tokens between Web services. WS-Trust is an extension to WS-Security that provides methods for issuing, renewing, and validating security tokens as well as methods for establishing and brokering trust relationships between Web services. If the requester does not supply appropriate claims, it can use the security policy declared by WS-SecurityPolicy to determine the URI of the provider's Security Token Service (STS), who can provide the requester with the appropriate claims. Additionally, WS-Trust supports multi-messaging exchanges, allowing providers to use a challenge-response mechanism for authorization. Because WS-Trust builds upon WS-Security, claims can be anything from a digital signature to a X.509 certificate or an XML-based token such as a SAML assertion.

WS-Federation expands on WS-Trust by providing various protocols by which STSs (interchangeably called Identity Providers in WS-Federation), requesters, and providers can interact with one another to allow Web services to trust each other across organizational boundaries. Each organization is a separate *trust realm*. WS-Federation allows Web services to communicate between multiple trust realms. Additionally, WS-Federation provides two profiles for how requesters interact with providers and STSs: the active requester profile and the passive requester profile. The passive requester profile details how messages should be passed between a requester Web browser, the provider, the Identity Providers (IPs) and STSs of both organizations so that WS-Federation can be used within the context of Web applications, providing users with a single sign-on experience. The active requester profile details how requesters should interact with the provider and the IP/STSs to access a provider in another trust realm.

---

33 A summary of the Liberty Alliance Identity Web Services Framework can be found in the *Liberty ID-WSF Overview v 1.1*, available at http://www.projectliberty.org/liberty/content/download/1307/8286/file/liberty-idwsf-overview-v1.1.pdf.

3.4 Describing Web Services Policies (WS-Policy)

WSDL describes how to communicate with a Web service by detailing the protocol bindings and message formats the Web service expects. In many cases, knowledge of protocol bindings and message formats is not sufficient for requesters to dynamically bind to the provider. WSDL is limited to describing what needs to be placed in the message itself; it does not specify what type of metadata should be supplied, such as how the message will be authenticated or what portions of the message should be signed. To this end, Microsoft, IBM, BEA and others developed the Web Services Policy (WS-Policy) Framework, which allows providers to express the capabilities, requirements and characteristics of the Web service.

WS-Policy requirements can range from specific on-the-wire requirements, such as requiring WS-Security encryption and signatures, to more abstract requirements, such as QoS or privacy requirements. A WS-Policy *policy expression* can provide senders with the essential metadata to fully automate the task of dynamic binding. A policy expression contains a set of policy alternatives encompassing sets of assertions.

Policy assertions are defined for a number of WS-* specifications, including WS-SecurityPolicy, WS-ReliableMessaging Policy Assertion (WS-RM Policy) and WS-Addressing WSDL Binding. The WS-Policy Primer[34] defines how these specifications can be used within a policy expression. As of mid-2007, there are three primary specifications defining WS-Policy assertions:

- WS-SecurityPolicy defines assertions to specify integrity, confidentiality, and information about security tokens.
- WS-RM Policy defines assertions that can be used to specify how a Web service uses WS-ReliableMessaging.
- WS-Addressing WSDL Binding defines elements that can be used within a WSDL descriptor to specify the use of WS-Addressing.

Figure 3-2 shows a sample WS-Policy expression.[35]

```
<Policy>
  <All>
    <wsap:UsingAddressing/>
    <sp:TransportBinding>
      <All>
        <sp:TransportToken>
          <Policy>
            <sp:HttpsToken RequireClientCertificate="true"/>
          </Policy>
        </sp:TransportToken>
        <sp:AlgorithmSuite>
          <Policy>
            <sp:Basic256Sha256Rsa15/>
          </Policy>
        </sp:AlgorithmSuite>
      </All>
    </sp:TransportBinding>
  </All>
</Policy>
```

Figure 3-2. Sample WS-Policy Expression

34 *WS-Policy Primer* is available at http://www.w3.org/TR/ws-policy-primer.

35 The examples used in this section are based on those provided by the *WS-Policy Primer*.

The root expression of the example in Figure 3-2 is an *All* tag, which is used to specify that all of the contained expressions must be met by the requester for it to comply with the provider policy. The *All* tag contains the following expressions:

- *wsap:UsingAddressing*, which specifies that requesters should include WS-Addressing information in the SOAP header.
- *sp:TransportBinding*, which specifies that requesters should use TLS to secure the SOAP message and defines the required parameters.

The *sp:TransportBinding* element contains an *All* tag containing two expressions:

- *sp:TransportToken*, which specifies what type of token the sender must provide. In this example, *sp:HttpsToken* indicates that senders must provide a client certificate through TLS.
- *sp:AlgorithmSuite* specifies what algorithms the sender's TLS library must support. In this example, *sp:Basic256Sha256Rsa15*, defined by WS-SecurityPolicy, is used to indicate that the Advanced Encryption Standard (AES) algorithm should be used with a key size of 256 bits for symmetric cryptography, the 256-bit Secure Hash Algorithm (SHA) should be used for hashing, and version 1.5 of the RSA encryption algorithm for asymmetric cryptography.

WS-Policy can also be used to describe the parameters necessary when using WS-ReliableMessaging to ensure message delivery. Figure 3-3 shows a policy defining an inactivity timeout of 2 seconds, a base retransmission interval of 5 seconds using the exponential backoff algorithm and an acknowledgement interval of 5 seconds.

```
<Policy>
  <wsrm:RMAssertion>
    <All>
      <wsrm:InactivityTimeout Milliseconds="2000"/>
      <wsrm:BaseRetransmissionInterval Milliseconds="5000"/>
      <wsrm:ExponentialBackoff/>
      <wsrm:AcknowledgementInterval Milliseconds="5000"/>
    </All>
  </wsrm:RMAssertion>
</Policy>
```

Figure 3-3. Sample WS-ReliableMessaging Policy Expression

Receivers have the option of specifying whether senders should use TLS or WS-Security to secure SOAP messages. Some receivers may wish to let senders decide which option to support. In this case, the *ExactlyOne* expression would be used to indicate the option in a manner similar to Figure 3-4.

```
<Policy>
  <ExactlyOne>
      <sp:TransportBinding>...</sp:TransportBinding>
      <All>
        <sp:SignedParts>
          <All>
            <sp:Body/>
            <sp:Header/>
          </All>
        </sp:SignedParts>
        <sp:EncryptedParts>
          <Policy>
            <sp:Body/>
          </Policy>
        </sp:EncryptedParts>
      </All>
  </ExactlyOne>
</Policy>
```

Figure 3-4. Sample WS-Policy Expression Using ExactlyOne

The *ExactlyOne* expression in Figure 3-4 contains two expressions related to securing Web service messages between the requester and provider. Senders must choose exactly one of these options when sending a SOAP message to this service:

- *sp:TransportBinding*, which indicates requesters may use SSL/TLS to secure messages
- *All*, which contains two WS-SecurityPolicy expressions that must be followed when using WS-Security in place of SSL/TLS:
  - *sp:SignedParts*, which indicates that both the SOAP message body and header must be signed
  - *sp:EncryptedParts,* which indicates that the SOAP message body must be encrypted.

Each policy expression can contain an *All* expression, an *ExactlyOne* expression or a policy expression element from a WS-Policy grammar, such as WS-Security, WS-RM, or WS-Addressing. Each of these expressions may contain another Policy expression. This level of flexibility allows providers to completely specify the requirements that must be met by requesters beyond those described in the provider's WSDL description.

Policy expressions are external to the metadata stored in UDDI and WSDL, so providers must rely on a separate mechanism for distributing WS-Policy information: WS-MetadataExchange or WS-PolicyAttachment. The WS-MetadataExchange specification defines an encapsulation format for Web service metadata (such as WS-Policy expressions), a mechanism for metadata-driven message exchange, and relies on the WS-Transfer specification to provide a Web service endpoint from which requesters can retrieve the metadata. The WS-PolicyAttachment specification defines how to reference policies from WSDL definitions, how to associate policies with deployed endpoints, and how to associate policies with UDDI entries.

In 2006, WS-Policy and WS-PolicyAttachment were submitted to W3C for standardization. They are scheduled to be released as W3C Recommendations in 2007. In 2005, WS-SecurityPolicy was submitted to the OASIS Web Services Secure Exchange Technical Committee. Even though these specifications are not official OASIS standards, interoperable commercial and open source implementations are available from organizations that were not involved in developing the specification, such as the Apache Software Foundation and Sun Microsystems.

3.5 Distributed Authorization and Access Management

Given the distributed nature of Web services architectures, managing authorization and access control credentials for users in a SOA environment can be challenging. Section 3.5 describes a number of traditional and emerging models and practices that may be extended to capture, manage, and enforce access control decisions for authorized users.

3.5.1 Authorization Models

The following subsections describe the authorization models most relevant to access management in a SOA, namely role-based, attribute-based, policy-based, and risk-adaptive access control. While role-based access control models may be familiar to most software designers and developers, knowledge of the other models can provide a perspective on the direction in which Web services access management is heading.

3.5.1.1 Role-Based Access Control

Role-based access control (RBAC) is an authorization mechanism that associates a set of access privileges with a particular role, often corresponding to a job function. With RBAC, all user access is mediated through roles. RBAC simplifies security management by providing a role hierarchy structure. In addition, RBAC has extensive provisions for constraints on user access based on administrator-defined relationships. This feature makes it possible to implement complex controls such as separation of duty. Constraints can include either static or dynamic attributes. Most commercially available RBAC systems conform to some of the RBAC standards, which are summarized on the NIST RBAC Web site.[36] Additionally, OASIS provides the *Core and hierarchical role based access control profile of XACML*, allowing organizations to support RBAC using the flexible and platform-independent XACML specification.[37]

In most cases, COTS Web servers or Web service platforms will support designation and assignment of privileges to roles as part of their standard definition of user accounts and access control privileges. In worst cases, the administrator will have to create the necessary user groups, enroll the appropriate users, and assign them role-appropriate privileges.

RBAC on a Web service platform should be implemented at a minimum for the administrator, developers, and any other privileged accounts that will be required for the Web service to operate. The Web service platform must be configured to enforce separation of roles (i.e., not allowing a user assigned to one role to perform functions exclusively assigned to another role). The privileges associated with each role should be assigned in a way that implements *least privilege*—each role should be assigned only the minimum privileges needed to perform the functions required by the role.

Most vendors implement some form of RBAC in their core Web services products. Another alternative is to implement or deploy RBAC at the Web services level, which is supported by a number of XML gateways and Web service vendors. However, the RBAC policies supported are less granular because a COTS product may need to be generic so it can support many different types of organizational policies.

---

36 *The NIST RBAC Web site* is available at http://csrc.nist.gov/rbac/.

37 The *Core and hierarchical role based access control profile of XACML* is available at http://docs.oasis-open.org/xacml/2.0/access_control-xacml-2.0-core-spec-os.pdf.

3.5.1.2 Attribute-Based Access Control (ABAC)

ABAC provides a mechanism for representing a subject's (either a user or application) access profile through a combination of the following attribute types:

- **Subject Attributes (S).** Associated with a subject that defines the identity and characteristics of that subject
- **Resource Attributes (R).** Associated with a resource, such as a Web service, system function, or data
- **Environment Attributes (E).** Describes the operational, technical, or situational environment or context in which the information access occurs.

ABAC policy rules are generated as Boolean functions of *S, R,* and *E* attributes and dictate whether a subject S can access a resource R in a particular environment E - as loosely indicated in Figure 3-5:[38]

$$\begin{aligned} Rule\ X: can\_access(s, r, e) \leftarrow \\ f(ATTR(s), ATTR(r), ATTR(e)) \end{aligned}$$

Figure 3-5. ABAC Policy Function

ABAC clearly provides an advantage over traditional RBAC when extended into SOA environments, which can be extremely dynamic in nature. ABAC policy rules can be custom-defined with consideration for semantic context and are significantly more flexible than RBAC for fine-grained alterations or adjustments to a subject's access profile. ABAC also integrates seamlessly with XACML, which relies on policy-defined attributes to make access control decisions.

One additional benefit to Web service implementations of ABAC lies in the nature of the loose definition of subjects. Because ABAC provides the flexibility to associate policy rules to any actor, it can be extended to Web service software agents as well. Figure 3-6 illustrates how an ABAC attribute authority (AA) can be integrated with a SAML framework. In this diagram, the AA generates attribute assertions, which contain all the attributes necessary for an access control decision based on an ABAC policy written in XACML. The PDP uses the attribute assertions, the authentication assertion, and the XACML policy to generate an authorization decision assertion. XACML is discussed in detail in Section 3.5.4.

[38] This example appears in Eric Yuan, Jin Tong: *Attribute Based Access Control: A New Access Control Approach for Service Oriented Architectures*, available at http://lotos.site.uottawa.ca/ncac05.

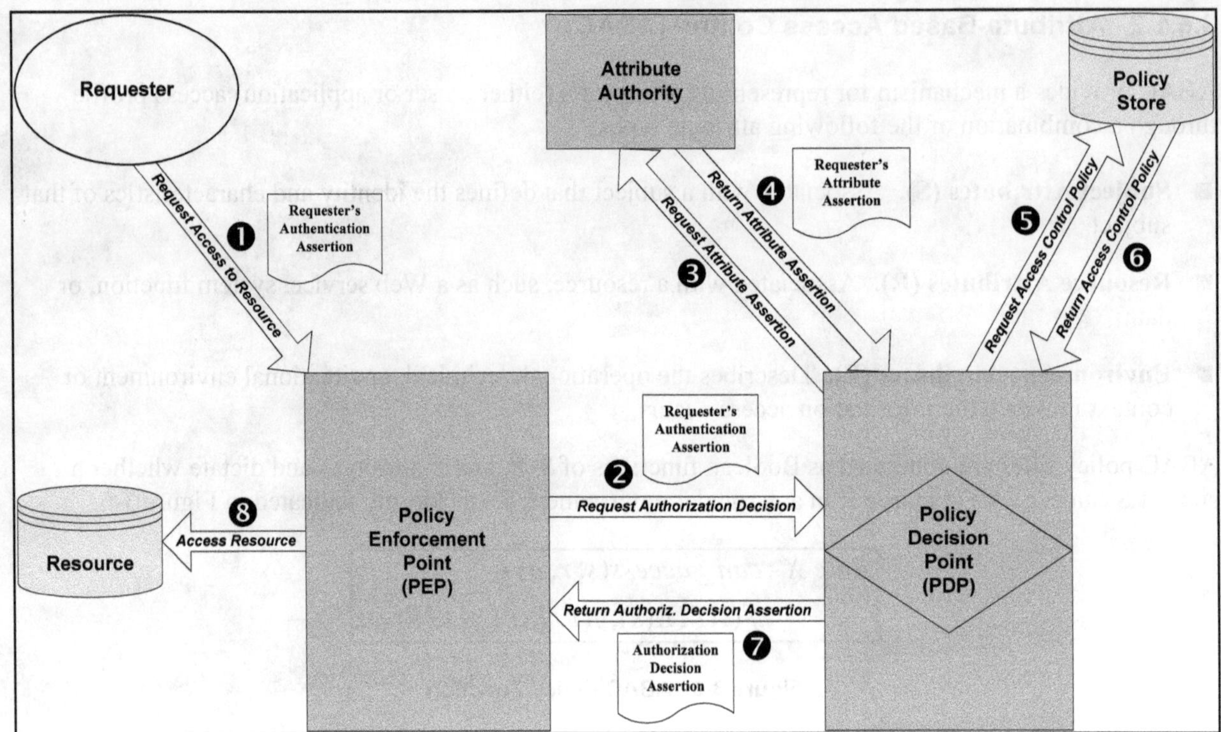

Figure 3-6. Use of SAML and XACML in Implementing ABAC

In Figure 3-6, the requester's authentication assertion is provided by the identity provider before accessing the resource. The following steps describe how SAML and XACML use the requester's attributes to determine whether access should be granted:

1. The requester attempts to access the resource and supply the authentication assertion.
2. The Policy Enforcement Point (PEP) sends a SAML authorization decision request to the PDP.
3. The PDP requests certain attribute assertions that are associated with the requester.
4. The AA returns the appropriate attribute assertions.
5. The PDP requests the XACML policy from the policy store.
6. The PDP receives the XACML policy.
7. After querying the XACML policy, the PDP sends an authorization decision assertion to the PEP.
8. Based on the authorization decision assertion, the PEP grants the requester access to the resource.

3.5.1.3 Policy-Based Access Control

Policy-based access control (PBAC) is a logical and somewhat bounded extension of ABAC that is useful for enforcing strict environment-level access control policies. PBAC introduces the notion of a policy authority, which serves as the access decision point for the environment in question. PBAC leverages the granular policy rule functions inherent to ABAC; it focuses more on automatically enforcing mandatory access controls (MAC), which are traditionally much more bounded than discretionary controls.

3.5.1.4 Risk Adaptive Access Control

Risk adaptive access control (RAdAC) is another variation on traditional access control methods. As opposed to RBAC, ABAC, and PBAC, however, RAdAC makes access control decisions on the basis of a relative risk profile of the subject and not necessarily strictly on the basis of a predefined policy rule. Figure 3-7 illustrates the logical process governing RAdAC, which uses a combination of a measured level of risk the subject poses and an assessment of operational need as the primary attributes by which the subject's access rights are determined.

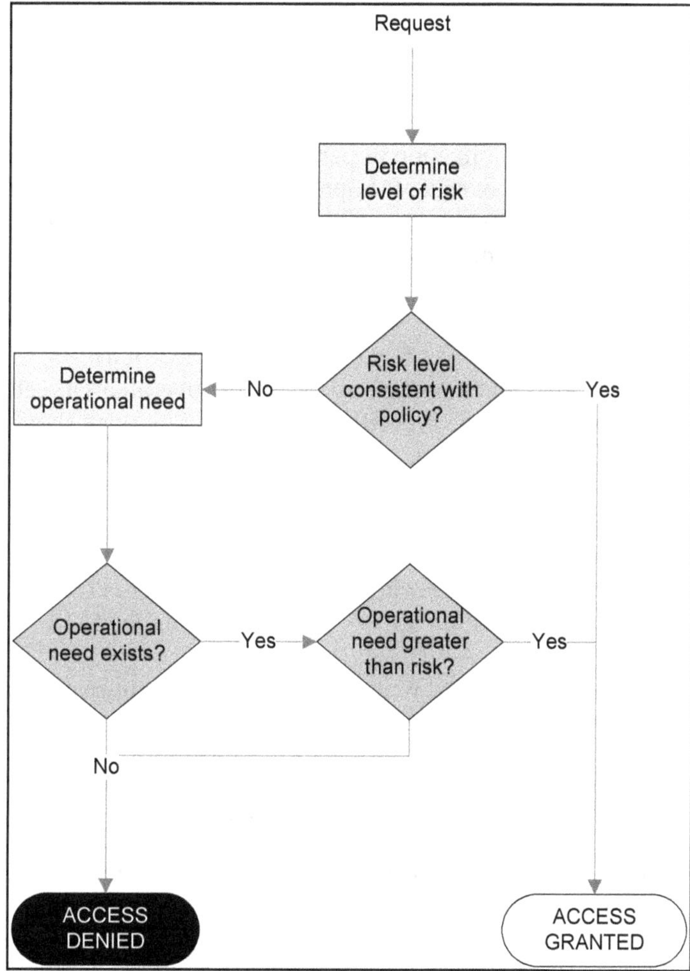

Figure 3-7. RAdAC Decision Tree

As a policy-driven mechanism, RAdAC is ostensibly an abstraction of PBAC. Unlike PBAC, however, a RAdAC framework requires associations with sources that are able to provide real-time, situation aware information upon which risk can be assessed with each authentication request.

3.5.2 Enforcing Least Privilege for Services

Trust and privilege are not synonymous. This said, trusted objects are often used to perform privileged functions. Least privilege can and should be applied regardless of what access control methodology is in use. In a Web services environment, each Web service should be designed to not request or expect to obtain privileges that exceed the minimum privileges it needs to perform its current operation.

Because of the functions they perform, trusted objects often require higher privileges than untrusted objects. Regardless of whether an object is trusted or untrusted, a privilege should be granted to it only at the moment the object needs that privilege, and the object should relinquish the privilege as soon as it completes the function/access for which the privilege was needed. Objects should not be allowed to retain a privilege that they are not actively using. Privileges should never be granted in anticipation of their being needed to perform some function/access in the future.

The application's design should ensure that only a minimal number of application objects need to be trusted or are ever granted privileges that exceed those of the end users that are associated with those objects. Whenever possible, implement objects without privileges, and if necessary, divide the complex functions they must perform into multiple simple functions, with a separate minimal required privilege for each function.

The application should also support minimization of permissions granted to a user, with each user granted only those minimal privileges needed to execute the application and access the data/resources for which the user is authorized. In most cases, user privileges will be determined by the user's role. As with other application objects, user privileges should be assigned at the moment they are needed, and revoked as soon as they are no longer being used.

Web services should be designed so that only a few components perform trusted operations. By restricting trusted functions to a small number of components, the overall architecture is simplified and the potential attack scenarios are minimized. Nevertheless, trusted functions should not be limited solely to a single component, which introduces a single point of failure. If the single trusted component fails, none of the dependent components will be able to function adequately, leading to a loss of availability. Trusted Web services should be deployed to be as available as possible.

There are three important concepts to consider when developing the access control policy for Web services. These concepts apply equally within the OS itself and within the SOA as a whole.

- **Separation of Duties.** Developers should write Web services to require only appropriate system roles or attributes to operate correctly.
- **Separation of Roles and Separation of Privileges**. The roles or attributes required for Web services should directly correspond to the set of functions to be performed.
- **Separation of Domains (Compartmentalization).** Access control policy may benefit from separating Web services into various compartments. For example, separating roles associated with rate service A from those associated with rate service B will allow an administrator to modify each service's permissions separately. The difficulty of compartmentalization depends on the access control mechanism used: this could be implemented in ABAC using resource attributes or through additional roles in RBAC.

Note that most general purpose operating systems' access controls cannot isolate intentionally cooperating programs. If the cooperation of malicious programs is a concern, the application should be implemented on a system which implements mandatory access controls and limits covert channels.

3.5.3 SAML

SAML defines an XML vocabulary for sharing security assertions that specify whether and how an entity was authenticated, information about an entity's attributes or whether an entity is authorized to perform a particular action. These assertions enable identity federation and distributed authorization within a SOA.

3.5.3.1 SAML Assertions

The SAML specification defines a framework for creating and exchanging generic assertions with given validity periods, signatures, encrypted elements and unique identifiers (among other attributes). Assertions are associated with a given *subject* (a named entity). When using SAML, there are two parties: the relying party and the asserting party. The asserting party asserts information about a particular subject, such as whether or not a user has been authenticated or has a particular attribute. The relying party uses the information supplied by the asserting party to make decisions, including, but not limited to, whether or not to trust the asserting party's assertion. By trusting the asserting party's information, the relying party can provide services without requiring the principal to authenticate again.

SAML assertions contain a number of required elements (except where otherwise noted):

- **ID**. Uniquely identifies this assertion
- **IssueInstant**. Timestamp indicating when the SAML assertion was created
- **Issuer**. Information about the entity that created the assertion
- **Signature**. Digital signature of the SAML assertion (optional)
- **Subject**. Information about the entity to which this assertion applies (optional)
- **Conditions**. Information used to determine the validity of the assertion, such as a validity period (optional)
- **Advice**. Information that may be useful in processing the assertion (optional)
- **Statements**. SAML statements can provide information about subject authentication, authorization decision or attributes. Additional types of statements can be defined by an extension. (optional)

Figure 3-8 shows a SAML assertion containing a single authentication statement. This assertion indicates that John Doe was authenticated on January 15, 2007 at 14:15:07 UTC via X.509 certificate and that this assertion is valid for one hour from the initial time of authentication.

```
<saml:Assertion xmlns:saml="urn:oasis:names:tc:SAML:2.0:assertion"
  Version="2.0"
  IssueInstant="2007-01-15T14:15:07Z">
  <saml:Issuer Format=urn:oasis:names:SAML:2.0:nameid-format:entity>
    http://issuer.example.com
  </saml:Issuer>
  <saml:Subject>
    <saml:NameID
      Format="urn:oasis:names:tc:SAML:1.1:nameid-format:x509SubjectName">
        CN=Doe.John, OU=NIST, O=U.S.  Government, C=US
    </saml:NameID>
  </saml:Subject>
  <saml:Conditions
    NotBefore="2007-01-15T14:15:07Z"
    NotOnOrAfter="2007-01-15T15:15:07Z">
  </saml:Conditions>
  <saml:AuthnStatement
    AuthnInstant="2005-01-15T14:15:07Z">
    <saml:AuthnContext>
      <saml:AuthnContextClassRef>
        urn:oasis:names:tc:SAML:2.0:ac:classes:X509
      </saml:AuthnContextClassRef>
    </saml:AuthnContext>
  </saml:AuthnStatement>
</saml:Assertion>
```

Figure 3-8. SAML Assertion

In addition to having digital signatures, SAML assertions may be encrypted using the *EncryptedAssertion* element, preventing third party entities from viewing the assertion.

3.5.3.2 SAML Statements

SAML defines three types of statements—authentication, attribute, and authorization—allowing SAML assertions to provide a wealth of information about individual subjects.

SAML authentication statements indicate that a subject was authenticated and provide specific details, such as what authentication method was used, when the authentication occurred, and who the authenticating entity was. Different techniques for establishing identity are supported, ranging from use of a password to use of hardware tokens and personal physical attributes (biometrics). SAML allows assertions to specify any type of authentication mechanism used and provides a vocabulary for a number of commonly used mechanisms. Figure 3-8 shows a sample authentication statement.

A SAML authorization decision statement may be used to assert that a request by a subject to access a specified resource has resulted in the specified decision and may optionally include evidence to support the decision.

SAML attribute statements provide information about a particular subject that may be useful or necessary for determining whether or not access should be granted. In an RBAC environment, a SAML attribute statement can provide information about the subject's roles; similarly, in an ABAC environment, a SAML attribute statement can provide the attributes required by the policy.

3.5.3.3 SAML Protocols

The SAML specification defines the SAML protocol, an XML-based request and response protocol for processing SAML assertions.[39] The SAML binding specification describes how to embed SAML

[39] More information about SAML protocols is available via *SAML Assertions and Protocols* at http://docs.oasis-open.org/security/saml/v2.0/saml-core-2.0-os.pdf.

requests and responses within HTTP and SOAP, allowing SAML to support both traditional Web applications and Web services.

As shown in Figure 3-9 below, SAML requests contain the following required information (unless otherwise specified):

- ID: uniquely identifies the SAML request
- IssueInstant: a timestamp indicating when the request was made
- Destination: a URI representing the receiver of the SAML request (optional)
- Consent: indicates whether or not the principal's consent was obtained for the request (optional)
- Issuer: identifies the sender (optional)
- Signature: a digital signature of the request (optional)
- Extensions: optional extensions, such as the *XACMLPolicyQuery* element defined by the XACML 2.0 SAML Profile (optional)

```
<samlp:AuthnRequest
  xmlns:samlp="urn:oasis:names:tc:SAML:2.0:protocol"
  xmlns:saml="urn:oasis:names:tc:SAML:2.0:assertion"
  Version="2.0"
  ID="2b67a31b17b64aff9827281f0c8eb25b"
 IssueInstant="2007-01-15T15:00:00Z"
 Destination="https://www.nist.gov/identityprovider/">
  <saml:Issuer>http://csrc.nist.gov/</saml:Issuer>
  <saml:Subject>
    <saml:NameID
      Format="urn:oasis:names:tc:SAML:1.1:nameid-format:x509SubjectName">
        CN=Doe.John, OU=NIST, O=U.S. Government, C=US
    </saml:NameID>
  </saml:Subject>
  <samlp:RequestedAuthnContext>
    <saml:AuthnContextClassRef>
      urn:oasis:names:tc:SAML:2.0:ac:classes:X509
    </saml:AuthnContextClassRef>
  <samlp:RequestedAuthnContext>
  <samlp:NameIDPolicy
    Format="urn:oasis:names:tc:SAML:1.1:nameid-format:X509"
  </samlp:NameIDPolicy>
</samlp:AuthnRequest>
```

Figure 3-9. SAML Protocol Request

As shown in Figure 3-10 below, SAML responses contain similar information (required unless otherwise specified):

- ID
- InResponseTo: the ID of the corresponding request (optional)
- IssueInstant
- Destination (optional)
- Consent (optional)
- Issuer (optional)

- Signature (optional)
- Extensions (optional)
- Status: a code representing the status of the response (optional).

```
<samlp:Response
  xmlns:samlp="urn:oasis:names:tc:SAML:2.0:protocol"
  xmlns:saml="urn:oasis:names:tc:SAML:2.0:assertion"
  Version="2.0"
  ID="df57420e8a724e3188d4d81e68f7a97f"
  IssueInstant="2007-01-15T15:01:42Z"
  InResponseTo="2b67a31b17b64aff9827281f0c8eb25b">
  <saml:Issuer>http://www.nist.gov/</saml:Issuer>
  <samlp:Status>
    <samlp:StatusCode Value="urn:oasis:names:tc:SAML:2.0:status:Success"/>
  </samlp:Status>
  <saml:Assertion xmlns:saml="urn:oasis:names:tc:SAML:2.0:assertion"
    Version="2.0"
    IssueInstant="2007-01-15T14:15:07Z">
    <saml:Issuer Format=urn:oasis:names:SAML:2.0:nameid-format:entity>
      http://issuer.example.com
    </saml:Issuer>
    <saml:Subject>
      <saml:NameID
        Format="urn:oasis:names:tc:SAML:1.1:nameid-format:x509SubjectName">
          CN=Doe.John, OU=NIST, O=U.S. Government, C=US
      </saml:NameID>
    </saml:Subject>
    <saml:Conditions
      NotBefore="2007-01-15T14:15:07Z"
      NotOnOrAfter="2007-01-15T15:15:07Z">
    </saml:Conditions>
    <saml:AuthnStatement
      AuthnInstant="2005-01-15T14:15:07Z">
      <saml:AuthnContext>
        <saml:AuthnContextClassRef>
          urn:oasis:names:tc:SAML:2.0:ac:classes:X509
        </saml:AuthnContextClassRef>
      </saml:AuthnContext>
    </saml:AuthnStatement>
  </saml:Assertion>
</samlp:Response>
```

Figure 3-10. SAML Response

SAML requests and responses are extended by each of the SAML protocols, providing support for a variety of SAML use cases. The SAML specification defines six protocols, allowing extensions to provide support for future protocols.

The *assertion query and request protocol* allows services to request specific assertions from a SAML authority. Services can request an assertion based on its ID, or query for authentication, attribute or authorization decision assertions.

The *authentication request protocol* allows services to request that an entity be authenticated by the identity provider; the subject may be authenticated before, during, or after the identity provider receives the authentication request. The authentication request protocol can play an important role in authenticating users in a seamless fashion when traversing from a publicly available service to a protected service. Similarly, the authentication request protocol can support re-authenticating subjects or requiring stronger authentication when accessing sensitive services.

The *artifact resolution protocol* allows a SAML provider to retrieve a SAML message based on its artifact, which is a reference to the message. The SAML-aware service passes the artifact to the provider instead of the SAML message itself. Artifacts are intended to be used when the transport mechanism has size constraints or cannot provide a secure channel through which to send a SAML message. For example, a SAML artifact can be passed as an HTTP GET parameter, allowing a traditional Web browser to pass a SAML assertion from the identity provider to a Web application without requiring the Web browser to be SAML-compliant.

The *name identifier management protocol* provides a mechanism through which SAML identity providers and service providers can notify one another that a principal's identifier has a new or modified value or format. Identity providers supply a *ManageNameIDRequest* element containing a *NameID* or *EncryptedNameID* element and *NewID*, *NewEncryptedID*, or *Terminate* element. Privacy concerns may be met by submitting the identifiers in encrypted form. Through the *Terminate* element, an identity provider can inform service providers that it will no longer supply assertions for the specified principal, or a service provider can inform the identity provider that it will no longer accept assertions for the specified principal.

The *single logout protocol* allows a principal to simultaneously log out of multiple sessions from a single service provider. When a principal has authenticated to an identity provider, the identity provider may initiate a session so that the principal does not need to re-authenticate (the identity provider becomes a session authority). When the principal accesses service providers, they may wish to initiate sessions to alleviate the need to communicate with the identity provider for each of the principal's requests (the service provider becomes a session participant). Should the principal wish to terminate all sessions associated with the initial authentication, a *LogoutRequest* may be sent to any of the session participants. If a session participant received the *LogoutRequest*, it will forward the *LogoutRequest* to the session authority. The session authority will send a *LogoutRequest* to all session participants except for the participant that initiated the *LogoutRequest*. The single logout protocol ensures that the principal does not need to be aware of all sessions associated with the original authentication.

The *name identifier mapping protocol* allows a provider to request a principal's name identifier from an identity provider in a specific format. A service provider must send a *NameIDMappingRequest* to the identity provider with a *BaseID*, *NameID* or *EncryptedID* element identifying the principal and a *NameIDPolicy* element indicating the format of the identifier to be returned. Use of an *EncryptedID* element can ensure that the principal's privacy is adequately maintained during the exchange. The identity provider will return a *NameID* or *EncryptedID* that satisfies the request parameters.

3.5.3.4 SAML Profiles

The SAML specification provides a number of profiles[40] that specify how SAML messages, assertions and protocols are to be used in various contexts. Because SAML is a versatile specification, there are five categories of profiles. Some categories only define a single profile, leaving room for future SAML specifications to expand. The five profile categories are:

- **Single sign-on (SSO).** These profiles define the protocols necessary to support SSO across multiple Web applications. There are profiles defining how to support SAML SSO when the client uses a

[40] More information about SAML protocols is available via *SAML Assertions and Protocols* at http://docs.oasis-open.org/security/saml/v2.0/saml-profiles-2.0-os.pdf.

Web browser or a SAML-aware client or proxy, a profile for discovery identity providers, a profile for single logout, and a profile for managing identifiers among multiple service providers.

- **Artifact resolution**. This profile defines how SAML-aware providers should retrieve the SAML assertion associated with a SAML artifact provided by a requester.
- **Assertion query/request**. This profile describes how to use the SAML assertion query/request protocol over a synchronous protocol, such as SOAP.
- **Name identifier mapping**. This profile describes how to use the SAML name identifier mapping protocol.
- **Attribute**. These profiles define how to represent attributes from common attribute stores in SAML assertions.

3.5.3.5 SAML Attributes

In Web services, attributes are usually disseminated using either SAML attribute assertions or X.509 certificates containing the required attributes. While X.509 certificates only provide a limited set of attributes, SAML attributes can encompass any type of attribute. In most enterprise systems, user attributes are stored in various Lightweight Directory Access Protocol (LDAP) or X.500 directories, Relational Data Base Management Systems (RDBMS), or Active Directories (AD). In the SAML architecture, these are referred to as *attribute stores*. By abstracting the various forms of attribute stores into a single entity, the SAML request/response protocol can be used to query any attribute store, regardless of its underlying structure.

Through the SAML attribute profiles, interoperability between the attribute store's SAML interface and the Web service accessing it is guaranteed. SAML V2.0 provides attribute profiles for X.500/LDAP attributes, Universally Unique Identifiers (UUID), DCE PAC attributes, and XACML attributes. The X.500/LDAP, UUID, and DCE PAC attribute profiles detail how to convert between SAML attributes and the structures of the individual attribute stores. While XACML is not an attribute store, the XACML attributes profile details how SAML assertions can be used as input to XACML authorization decisions. SAML can be extended to support any other form of attribute store, allowing attributes to be accessed in a Web services environment.

While SAML provides a mechanism for accessing attributes, it does not provide a mechanism for updating attributes in a SOA. As of this writing, there is no Web services standard for modifying the contents of data stores used by a SOA. For Web services to alter the contents of the various attribute stores, custom Web services would have to be developed using appropriate WS-Security and authorization techniques.

3.5.3.6 SAML Security

The *Security and Privacy Considerations for the OASIS Security Assertion Markup Language*[41] document[42] outlines the threats faced when using SAML and provides guidance in securing a SAML-based architecture. In particular, it is important to recognize that once a SAML assertion has been issued, it is not possible to control its dissemination. An entity that receives a SAML assertion may pass it on to other, potentially malicious entities as part of the system. It is important to ensure that all SAML

---

41 *Security and Privacy Considerations for the OASIS Security Assertion Markup Language* is available at http://www.oasis-open.org/committees/download.php/3404/oasis-sstc-saml-sec-consider-1.1.pdf.

42 The *Security and Privacy Considerations for the OASIS Security Assertion Markup Language* is available at http://docs.oasis-open.org/security/saml/v2.0/saml-sec-consider-2.0-os.pdf.

assertions and entities that will receive them follow appropriate organizational policies. Because of this, it is possible that a malicious entity may attempt to use SAML assertions in replay attacks (in particular, authentication assertions and authorization decision assertions are likely to be replayed). There are a number of techniques that can mitigate this threat, including:

- Encrypting the assertion will prevent a third party from viewing it, although a malicious entity may attempt to resend the encrypted assertion.
- Signing the entire message rather than the assertion itself, using WS-Security in a SOAP response or SSL/TLS in a HTTP response. This way, an attacker must resend the whole message to be successful.
- Enforcing validity periods and ensuring that the IssueInstant of the assertion is reasonable. This will minimize the amount of time during which an attacker may successfully execute a replay attack.

If a SAML authority is publicly accessible, an attacker may send SAML queries to gain information about the subjects within the system. Similarly, an attacker may construct a malicious SAML authority. In each case, it is especially important that entities using SAML authenticate one another before requesting or providing information about subjects within the SOA.

3.5.4 XACML

Within Web services extensions, a vocabulary is required for expressing the rules needed to make authorization decisions. One such vocabulary is XACML. XACML is a language- and platform-neutral method for representing and enforcing security policies. Using XML as a basis for a security policy language is the natural choice because its syntax can easily be extended to conform to the requirements of individual applications. XACML defines both a policy language and a request/response language for access control decisions. The policy language is used to define the access control requirements of a particular system or organization. The request/response language provides a mechanism for asking whether or not a particular action is allowed. XACML also defines a method for mapping the request to the policy and determining whether or not the policy allows the requested action.

XACML is used in conjunction with SAML to provide a means for standardizing access control decisions for resources over a network. XACML uses a context that can easily be mapped on SAML requests to determine if access should be granted to a resource based on XACML policies. Once the policy is evaluated and returns a true or false value to indicate whether or not access is granted, a SAML authorization decision assertion is returned, which is then processed accordingly.

The following subsections describe additional details on the XACML specification, including major inherent features and a discussion of how the transparent components of XACML operate in the background. Also provided are summaries on how XACML is implemented in a SOA and examples of practical extensions/implementations of XACML within the community.

3.5.4.1 How XACML Works

XACML defines a language for creating policies. The basic elements for policies are *Policy* and *PolicySet*. A PolicySet can contain Policies and references to external policies. A Policy defines a single access control policy that is expressed through one or more Rules. XACML defines several combining algorithms for determining a single decision from the results of multiple rules. Figure 3-11 shows an XACML policy that uses the permit-overrides combining policy in which any result of "permit" will grant access. This policy shows that members with a group attribute of "developers" can perform the read action on http://server.example.com/code/docs/guide.html.

```
<Policy PolicyId="ExamplePolicy"
 RuleCombiningAlgId="urn:oasis:names:tc:xacml:1.0:rule-combining-algorithm:permit-overrides">
  <Target>
    <Subjects> <AnySubject/> </Subjects>
    <Resources>
      <Resource>
        <ResourceMatch MatchId="urn:oasis:names:tc:xacml:1.0:function:anyURI-equal">
          <AttributeValue
DataType="http://www.w3.org/2001/XMLSchema#anyURI">http://server.example.com/code/docs/guide.
html</AttributeValue>
          <ResourceAttributeDesignator DataType="http://www.w3.org/2001/XMLSchema#anyURI"
           AttributeId="urn:oasis:names:tc:xacml:1.0:resource:resource-id"/>
        </ResourceMatch>
      </Resource>
    </Resources>
    <Actions> <AnyAction/> </Actions>
  </Target>
  <Rule RuleId="ReadRule" Effect="Permit">
    <Target>
      <Subjects> <AnySubject/> </Subjects>
      <Resources> <AnyResource/> </Resources>
      <Actions>
        <Action>
          <ActionMatch MatchId="urn:oasis:names:tc:xacml:1.0:function:string-equal">
            <AttributeValue
             DataType="http://www.w3.org/2001/XMLSchema#string">read</AttributeValue>
            <ActionAttributeDesignator DataType="http://www.w3.org/2001/XMLSchema#string"
             AttributeId="urn:oasis:names:tc:xacml:1.0:action:action-id"/>
          </ActionMatch>
        </Action>
      </Actions>
    </Target>
    <Condition FunctionId="urn:oasis:names:tc:xacml:1.0:function:string-equal">
      <Apply FunctionId="urn:oasis:names:tc:xacml:1.0:function:string-one-and-only">
        <SubjectAttributeDesignator DataType="http://www.w3.org/2001/XMLSchema#string"
         AttributeId="group"/>
      </Apply>
      <AttributeValue
       DataType="http://www.w3.org/2001/XMLSchema#string">developers</AttributeValue>
    </Condition>
  </Rule>
</Policy>
```

Figure 3-11. An XACML Policy

The XACML specification uses the term policy enforcement point (PEP) to refer to the entity that performs the access control, such as a file system or Web server. The PEP sends XACML requests to the PDP and receives XACML responses that it uses to grant or deny access. The PDP is the entity that receives access requests from the PEP. It looks at the request and the applicable policy and sends a response as to whether or not access should be granted.

Figure 3-12 shows an XACML request in which the user, jsmith@users.example.com, is attempting to perform a read action on http://server.example.com/docs/guide.html. This request provides the user's group attribute, which is required by the policy to make the access decision. From the request, jsmith@users.example.com's group attribute is "developers." This request is sent by the PEP to the PDP.

```
<Request>
  <Subject>
    <Attribute AttributeId="urn:oasis:names:tc:xacml:1.0:subject:subject-id"
     DataType="urn:oasis:names:tc:xacml:1.0:data-type:rfc822Name">
      <AttributeValue>jsmith@users.example.com</AttributeValue>
    </Attribute>
    <Attribute AttributeId="group"
     DataType="http://www.w3.org/2001/XMLSchema#string"
     Issuer="admin@users.example.com">
      <AttributeValue>developers</AttributeValue>
    </Attribute>
  </Subject>
  <Resource>
    <Attribute AttributeId="urn:oasis:names:tc:xacml:1.0:resource:resource-id"
     DataType="http://www.w3.org/2001/XMLSchema#anyURI">
      <AttributeValue>http://server.example.com/code/docs/guide.html</AttributeValue>
    </Attribute>
  </Resource>
  <Action>
    <Attribute AttributeId="urn:oasis:names:tc:xacml:1.0:action:action-id"
     DataType="http://www.w3.org/2001/XMLSchema#string">
      <AttributeValue>read</AttributeValue>
    </Attribute>
  </Action>
  <Environment/>
</Request>
```

Figure 3-12. An XACML Request.

Once the PDP receives the request, it processes the request against the policy provided in Figure 3-11. Because jsmith@users.example.com's group attribute is "developers", the resulting decision is "permit." This decision is sent to the PEP in the form of an XACML response as shown in Figure 3-13. The PEP will then permit jsmith@users.example.com to read http://server.example.com/code/docs/guide.html.

```
<Response>
  <Result>
    <Decision>Permit</Decision>
    <Status>
      <StatusCode Value="urn:oasis:names:tc:xacml:1.0:status:ok"/>
    </Status>
  </Result>
</Response>
```

Figure 3-13. An XACML Response

Access control policies are comprised of Targets and Rules. A *Target* defines a set of conditions for the Subject, Resource, and Action that must be met for a PolicySet, Policy, or Rule to apply to a request. The Target is used by the PDP to determine whether or not the request applies to this particular rule. Once an applicable policy is found, the Rules are activated. Most *Rules* consist of an Effect and a Condition. The Effect determines what the results of the Condition mean, while the Condition can test that any attribute meets a certain requirement.

Attributes are used in XACML to aid in creating access control policies. In essence, *attributes* refer to individual properties of the Subject, Resource, Action, or Environment that are applicable to the access request, such as the Subject's user name or the Environment's current time. A Policy uses the *AttributeDesignator* and the *AttributeSelector* to retrieve attributes from a request. The AttributeDesignator specifies an attribute with a given name and type that the PDP will retrieve from the request or some external source. AttributeSelectors provide an XPath query for resolving the values in the request or elsewhere. The attributes received are used in Rules to determine whether or not to grant access.

3.5.4.2 Using XACML

XACML does not have the inherent ability to control access to anything. It is used to provide an access control policy and to determine whether or not a requested action is allowed. The policy and requested action can be anything from read-access of a particular element in an XML file to a request for entry through a physical door. When using XACML in a Web service or Web application, it is important to understand that the application itself must be the PEP. All requests for information from the client or requester service must be translated into an access request. In many implementations, XACML is used solely for authentication, in which case only the authentication request needs to be translated while all subsequent requests would be allowed. As mentioned earlier, the PEP needs to send XACML requests to the PDP. The PDP will take the XACML request and determine the appropriate XACML response to send to the PEP, which will then grant or deny the request.

Because there is no mechanism for transmitting XACML over a network in the XACML specification, SAML is traditionally used to transmit requests, responses, and attributes over a network. SAML was designed for the secure exchange of authentication and authorization information, but not for performing the actual decisions. This makes it a perfect match for transmitting XACML information over a network. The PEP converts the XACML request into a SAML query and sends it to the PDP. The PDP converts the SAML query into an XACML request and processes the request against the XACML policy. The XACML response is converted into a SAML response and sent back to the PEP, which converts it back into an XACML response. SAML does not provide message confidentiality—only message integrity. If any of the data being transmitted is sensitive, it must be transmitted using SSL/TLS or WS-Security. If the SAML protocol is being used without SSL/TLS, all SAML messages must be signed appropriately.

The XACML v2.0 specification only supports a configuration where the PDP and PEP are on the same system. There is no standard specified for transmitting XACML policies, requests, or responses over a network. SAML is designed for the secure transmission of security attributes, which are used by XACML to determine whether or not to grant access. To this end, SAML v2.0 includes an XACML binding.

Because XACML can be used over a variety of languages and platforms, tools for generating XACML policies can be used for any application and platform that supports XACML, unlike current policy generators that only work with a specific application.

3.5.5 Role of XML Schema in Implementing Access Control

While not developed specifically for access control, XML schemas can be effective for controlling access to Web services. XML parsing libraries often support validating XML documents against a defined XML Schema. Because XML Schemas can rigidly define the types of data and format of XML elements, they can be used to prevent the Web service from processing invalid requests. For example, the SOAP XML Schema could be modified by a Web service developer to only allow portTypes that match a particular regular expression. All other requests would not pass through the XML validator and would not reach the Web service. In addition, the XML parser could be configured to use a different XML Schema based on the identity of the remote Web service, which would not require the developer to implement the necessary authorization functionality in the Web service itself. In fact, use of XML Schema-based access control could prove to be more powerful than programmatic access control since many malicious SOAP requests would not reach the application code. One of the drawbacks of using XML Schema validation for access control is that it could put a heavy load on the system, because Schema validation is processor-intensive; this could lead to a degradation of service.

3.5.6 Use of Specialized Security Metadata for Access Control

If the Web service handles personally identifiable information (PII), proprietary, or other sensitive data, it may need to label or otherwise mark output from the application. For labeling of Web pages, one approach is to use metatags to store the label information directly in the HTML source of the page, to be displayed as part of the page in the user's browser. If the Web page is printed from the browser, this label will be included in the printed output.

Some government agencies have defined XML-based markup syntax and schema for implementing security labels in data. The Intelligence Community (IC) Metadata Standards Working Group (MSWG) develops standards for affixing security labels to online XML and HTML content and downloadable electronic documents posted on the IC's Intelink World Wide Web-like intranet. While these standards are developed specifically for the IC, they can serve as a basis for any organization's metadata standards. In addition, any organization that interacts with the IC may improve communications efficiency by embracing these standards.

The IC security metadata standards are intended to be consistent with the key XML security standards (XML-Signature, XML-Encryption and XKMS). The relevant IC standards are:

- IC Metadata Standard for Publication (IC MSP)
- IC Metadata Standard for Information Security Markings (IC ISM)
- IC Standard for Core Metadata (IC Core).

Within DoD, a similar effort has been put forth called the DoD Discovery Metadata Standard (DDMS). DDMS does not directly support embedding metadata tags within XML documents. Instead, it focuses on creating metadata registries that can be accessed in conjunction with DoD resources. As with the IC standards, use of DDMS may improve efficiency in communications for organizations that interact closely with DoD.

The DoD and the IC are working on harmonization of security labels based on the labeling specifications defined by the IC's Controlled Access Program Coordination Office (CAPCO) and those based on DoD Directive 5200.1, *DoD Information Security Program* (13 December 1996).[43]

In the private sector, a number of organizations are developing metadata specifications to address regulations such as the Health Insurance Portability and Accountability Act (HIPAA) of 1996. The Food and Drug Administration (FDA) approved the Structured Product Labeling (SPL) specification from Health Level Seven (HL7) as a mechanism for exchanging medication information. SPL Release 2[44] provides confidentiality codes that can be used to specify whether a particular entity can view the information in the document.

The objective of these standards is to describe XML metadata tags and their possible values. These tags and values can be embedded in XML content to indicate the classification or sensitivity level associated with the tagged data. In addition, the standards describe one or more DTDs or XML Schemas specifying the rules for parsing the metadata security tags.

---

[43] For further information on DDMS, visit the DDMS page at http://www.afei.org/news/ddms.pdf.

[44] For further information on SPL, visit HL7's page at http://www.hl7.org.

3.6 Confidentiality and Integrity of Service to Service Interchanges

Although transport layer security mechanisms are provided through using secure transport protocols such as SSL/TLS, message layer security of XML is still needed for the following:

- **End-to-End Security.** Secure transport protocols can assure the security of messages only during transmission. Because messages are received and processed by intermediaries, secure end-to-end communication is not possible if these intermediaries are not completely trusted.
- **Transport Independence.** Even if all the communication links are secure and the intermediaries can be trusted, security information such as the authenticity of the originator of the message needs to be translated to the next secure transport protocol along the message path. This could be tedious and complex, which may lead to security breaches. It is important to deal with the security concerns at the message layer independently of the transport layers.
- **Security of Stored Messages.** Once a transmission is received and decrypted, transport layer security does not protect data from illicit accesses and alterations. In situations where messages are stored and then forwarded, message layer security is necessary.

The following subsections describe technologies that may be leveraged to improve the confidentiality and integrity of Web services. This includes both session/transport level security (i.e., SSL/TLS) as well as message-level security, such as that provided through WS-Security (as described below). Integrity can be enforced to an extent through the use of XML gateways (i.e., XML firewalls), and further explanation of this notion is provided in Section 3.6.4.

3.6.1 Transport Layer Confidentiality and Integrity: HTTPS

Because Web services rely on HTTP as the transport layer, they can be easily configured to communicate over HTTP Secure (HTTPS). The HTTPS protocol is defined as HTTP over SSL/TLS. SSL/TLS provide socket-layer security, encrypting all communication over a particular TCP connection—immediately granting an insecure application-layer protocol security without altering it. Through SSL/TLS, HTTPS supports authentication, confidentiality, and integrity of data sent between the endpoints. Use of HTTPS provides the following:

- Each service only needs to have knowledge of those services it directly communicates with, which reduces the certificate distribution problem.
- Each Web service uses the framework's authentication and authorization mechanism rather than implementation-specific code.

3.6.2 XML Confidentiality and Integrity

The XML security standards define a framework and processing rules that can be shared across applications using common tools, avoiding the need for extensive customization of applications to add security. The XML security standards reuse the concepts, algorithms and core technologies of legacy security systems while introducing changes necessary to support extensible integration with XML. This allows interoperability with a wide range of existing infrastructures and across deployments.

The XML security standards define XML vocabularies and processing rules using established cryptographic and security technologies, to provide flexible, extensible and practical ways of satisfying security requirements. The core XML security standards include the following:

- **XML Signature.** For integrity and signatures, XML Signature defines digital signatures and related cryptographic integrity and authentication measures for XML.
- **XML Encryption.** For confidentiality, XML Encryption supports encryption using a variety of both symmetric and asymmetric cryptographic algorithms.
- **XML Key Management Specification (XKMS).** For key management, XKMS addresses PKI and key management network services in XML.

Many other confidentiality and integrity technologies, such as SSL/TLS or virtual private networks (VPN), only provide confidentiality while the information is in transit, not while it is stored at a server. XML Encryption and XML Signature use the same cryptographic algorithms as other cryptographic technologies and may be subject to similar attacks. All applications depending on XML Encryption and XML Signature should follow the guidelines set forth in NIST SP 800-21-1[45], SP 800-32[46], SP 800-57[47], FIPS 140-2[48] and FIPS 186-2[49].

XKMS defines protocols for Public Key management services. Public Key management includes the creation of public and private key pairs, the binding of key pairs with identity and other attributes, and the representation of key pairs in different formats. Public key technology is essential to XML Signature, XML Encryption, and other security applications. When signing, the private key is used to sign and the public key is used to verify signatures. When encrypting, the public key is used to encrypt and the private key is used to decrypt. In both cases, the private key must be maintained under control of the owner and the public key may be shared with others. XKMS is designed to help manage the sharing of the public key to enable signature verification and encryption. XKMS enables users to delegate key management functions to a trust service accessed via SOAP and XML. XKMS enables key management to be provided as a service to the application, without having to use a PKI toolkit to implement the service.

When using XML Security standards in Web services, both the requester and provider must support the particular algorithms chosen and must decrypt or verify the SOAP messages before acting upon them. Also, because the SOAP specification does not provide support for encrypting portions of SOAP messages, both SOAP endpoints must understand the protocol and tags used to represent encrypted or signed SOAP elements. To prevent proprietary and incompatible Web service security mechanisms, the WS-Security standard was developed by Microsoft, IBM, and Verisign to define a unified mechanism for securing SOAP messages.

3.6.3 WS-Security for SOAP Confidentiality and Integrity

As mentioned earlier, the WS-Security standard was designed to use the XML Encryption and XML Signature specifications for message-layer confidentiality and integrity. By signing and encrypting at the message level, senders control whether intermediaries can modify or view the content in transit. Additionally, the entire message can be stored intact, maintaining integrity or confidentiality while at rest. Because message integrity is provided by digital signatures, non-repudiation can be achieved by logging individual messages for later retrieval (Section 3.7.2 describes non-repudiation in more detail). To fully

---

45 NIST SP 800-21-1, *Guideline for Implementing Cryptography in the Federal Government,* is available at http://csrc.nist.gov/publications/nistpubs/.

46 SP 800-32, *Introduction to Public Key Technology and the Federal PKI Infrastructure*, is available at http://csrc.nist.gov/publications/nistpubs/.

47 SP 800-57, *Special Publication on Key Management*, is available at http://csrc.nist.gov/publications/nistpubs/.

48 FIPS 140-2, *Security Requirements for Cryptographic Modules*, is available at http://csrc.nist.gov/publications/fips/.

49 FIPS 186-2, *Digital Signature Standard*, is available at http://csrc.nist.gov/publications/fips/.

support WS-Security, a Web service needs to be able to access public keys for all nodes with which it will interact, not simply those nodes it communicates with directly. This allows WS-Security to prevent man-in-the-middle attacks.

One of the main drawbacks associated with WS-Security is its use of asymmetric cryptographic algorithms for encryption, which are computationally intensive. To remedy this situation, the WS-SecureConversation specification was developed, allowing Web services to create a symmetric session key (similar to how SSL/TLS functions) to allow faster symmetric cryptographic algorithms to be used for message-level security. WS-SecureConversation is well-suited for Web services that receive or send large volumes of messages to a small number of services.

3.6.4 Role of XML Gateways in Integrity Protection

SOAP travels over HTTP, which is traditionally left open for Web traffic at perimeter firewalls. Additionally, with the advent of Liberty and SAML V2.0's Reverse SOAP (PAOS) specification, SOAP messages can pass through firewalls that limit incoming HTTP traffic but allow outgoing HTTP traffic. Some firewalls have begun to support blocking or allowing SOAP requests based on the source or destination of the request, but more robust and intelligent firewalls are needed to defend networks against malicious SOAP attacks.

To this end, XML gateways were developed to offer the functionality of application-level firewalls specifically for Web services. Application-aware firewalls are nothing new; they have been around in the form of HTTP proxies for HTTP-based traffic and allow organizations to limit what an application-layer protocol can and cannot do.

An XML gateway acts as the Web service and forwards all communication to the internal Web service, acting as an intermediary between untrusted services and the internal Web service. XML gateways can provide sophisticated authentication and authorization services, potentially improving the security of the Web service by having all SOAP messages pass through a hardened gateway before reaching any of the custom-developed code. XML gateways can restrict access based on source, destination, or WS-Security authentication tokens.

XML gateways also support schema validation and some offer support for SOAP intrusion prevention against the following attacks that target vulnerabilities native to XML and XML based services:

- **WSDL scanning.** Attempts to retrieve the WSDL of Web services to gain information that may be useful for an attack
- **Parameter tampering.** Modification of the parameters a Web service expects to receive in an attempt to bypass input validation and gain unauthorized access to some functionality
- **Replay attacks.** Attempts to resend SOAP requests to repeat sensitive transactions
- **Recursive/oversized payload attacks.** Attempts to perform a denial of service against the Web service by sending messages designed to overload the XML parser
- **External reference attacks.** Attempts to bypass protections by including external references that will be downloaded after the XML has been validated but before its processed by the application
- **Schema poisoning.** Supplying a schema with the XML document such that the XML validator will use the supplied schema, allowing a malicious XML document to be validated without error

- **Structured Query Language (SQL) injection.** Providing specially crafted parameters that will be combined within the Web service to generate a SQL query defined by the attacker
- **Buffer overflows.** Providing specially crafted parameters that will overload the input buffers of the application and will crash the Web service—or potentially allow arbitrary code to be executed.

Additionally, Web services behind an XML gateway may not need to implement the security functionality provided by the firewall, allowing developers to focus only on what the firewall does not support. Because SSL/TLS can be used between the firewall and the Web service, all communication between the Web service and the XML gateway can be trusted. If Web services behind the firewall do not implement security mechanisms to support confidentiality, integrity, and authentication, attackers that bypass the XML gateway may be able to subvert internal Web services. As such, it is always beneficial to implement defense-in-depth using XML gateways at the perimeter along with WS-Security or HTTPS for all internal Web services.

Finally, XML gateways support in-depth logging facilities for audit purposes. In conjunction with individual audit logs at each Web service, this allows administrators to keep track of what anomalies the XML gateway is experiencing to potentially fine-tune the XML gateway or notice when an attack has been successful and compromised an internal Web service. Nevertheless, the effectiveness of an XML gateway is dependent on the richness of the feature set and the granularity of policy control. Like any Web service, XML gateways are susceptible to threats from external attackers, so it is important to apply updates and define a policy for handling any intrusions related to the XML gateway.

3.7 Accountability End-to-End throughout a Service Chain

Because of the SOA property allowing Web services to dynamically bind to one another, it is difficult to implement accountability in a service chain. Auditing is essential in many transactions to be able to ensure, after the fact, that the transaction took place as expected. For example, financial transactions often require extensive auditing. The lack of auditing standards for Web services serves as the primary hindrance to effectively implementing accountability across a SOA.

In a SOA, auditing is accomplished by using a secure, distributed logging facility and WS-Security digital signatures. Through the use of a secure logging facility, all important WS-Security signed elements can be stored for audit purposes to determine which Web service performed what action. One common mechanism for implementing the logging facility is to develop Web service intermediaries that transparently log information about captured SOAP messages. Web services developed from scratch can be implemented to support an organization's distributed logging facility, but many COTS and government off-the-shelf (GOTS) Web services use their own non-standard logging mechanism. Standards efforts are on the horizon to enable interoperability between logging mechanisms, but until they are in place, organizations must support the wide variety of logging mechanisms in use.

Regardless of what logging mechanisms are in use within an organization, there is no way in a SOA to require all participants in a service chain to use WS-Security or logging. For example, one member of the service chain may not perform logging but may advertise that it does; while another member of the service chain does not support WS-Security but the service that accesses it performs signatures itself. It is important that the Web services a requester communicates with be trusted—and that trust should imply that each subsequent service in the chain will be held to the same standard of trust. When going through audit logs it will be apparent which member of a service chain did not follow the requirements of the SOA, as the required logs or signed elements will not be available for examination.

Enforcing accountability in a SOA (or other) environment requires the use of diligent auditing mechanisms, such that forensic data can be captured, compiled, and accurately attributed to users. The following subsections explain how auditing can be performed in SOAs. Section 3.7.2 explains the relevance of non-repudiation in a Web services environment and the means by which it can be enforced.

3.7.1 Audit in the SOA Environment

Most COTS Web servers include an audit or security event logging service that provides the application with the mechanism it needs to log security events to multiple destination logs. Configurable property-driven parameters allow the administrator to modify the semantics of the application's log data capture without needing to rewrite the application code. For example, Java's standard logging API provides an extensible event logging service for many Java applications. Logging and audit entries captured may be routed to the local operating system audit trail, or to audit middleware, using pluggable logging modules.

As noted, the audit/security event log data must be stored securely to prevent unauthorized tampering or disclosure of the log data. This secure storage may be implemented by channeling the log data via a secure connection to an external audit system, such as a central audit collection server, audit middleware, or the operating system audit trail. The audit/security event logs should be secured, either by transmitting the log data via an encrypted API, socket, or network connection, or by encrypting the log data before transferring them via an unencrypted or encrypted channel. In the case of a COTS audit server or audit middleware, the secure interface will ideally be provided as a standard feature of that product. If it is not, the application could provide it using a secure protocol or tunnel common to both it and the external audit system. Many organizations provide a logging core service within their SOA that other Web services can dynamically bind to securely submit logging data for storage in a central location. In addition to storing audit information on a remote system, it may be beneficial for Web services to store audit information locally in the event the central logging service fails or is temporarily inaccessible. NIST SP 800-92[50] provides guidance on managing security logs throughout an organization. While this guidance is not specific to SOA, many of the concepts introduced in the guide can be applied to Web services.

3.7.2 Non-Repudiation of Web Service Transactions

WS-Security provides non-repudiation services through its use of the XML Signature standard. Digital signatures can provide the necessary level of assurance required for non-repudiation. Through asymmetric encryption, each Web service has a unique key that can be used to sign SOAP elements. This signature can be verified by any subsequent Web service to verify which Web service performed the signature—and verify whether or not the signed element has changed, as a digital signature is only valid if the signed data remains unchanged.

WS-Security can provide non-repudiation of both the SOAP message itself and its contents. WS-Security supports signing the SOAP header, to ensure that the recipient and sender of the SOAP message have not changed since the message was sent. The SOAP message can be logged so that an audit can reveal that the SOAP message was valid. Additionally, sensitive information can be signed by another Web service for inclusion in the SOAP message. This allows a Web service to include signed data in different SOAP messages while maintaining that the original Web service signed the data—allowing the message sender to sign the SOAP header for a message that was originally sent by a different Web service. This can be particularly useful in Web service choreographies and orchestrations as the data may pass between a number of Web services before reaching its intended destination.

---

[50] NIST SP 800-92, *Guide to Computer Security Log Management*, is available at http://csrc.nist.gov/publications/nistpubs/.

3.8 Availability of Web Services

There is a close relationship between availability, QoS, and reliability. Availability is intended to ensure that QoS and reliability are maintained even when the Web service is subjected to intentional attempts to compromise its operation.

Where QoS is concerned with ensuring the Web service consistently operates at its expected level of performance, and reliability deals with ensuring the Web service continues to operate correctly and predictably in the presence of unintentional faults, availability ensures that:

- The Web service will continue to operate correctly and predictably in the presence of the types of intentionally-induced faults associated with DoS attacks
- If the Web service cannot avoid failing, it will not fail into an insecure state (i.e., its failure will not leave the service itself, its data, or its environment vulnerable to being compromised, subverted, or exploited to compromise something else) unless organizational policy requires the service to continue operating.

To achieve availability, a Web service must not only be designed and implemented to achieve QoS and reliability, but also to:

- Recognize and react to the attack patterns associated with DoS.
- When resistance is no longer possible, constrain and isolate the results of the DoS attack. This means preventing the DoS attack patterns from propagating beyond the point where they were first detected by the Web service.
- Recover and resume secure operation as soon as possible after a DoS.

It is particularly important that any planned performance degradations or orderly partial shutdowns not be extended to any of the service's security functions or self-protections. If the DoS attack becomes too persistent, or its propagation cannot be prevented, the entire Web service should shut down in a safe, secure manner. Unless a service is mission-critical as defined by organizational policy, it must never be allowed to continue operating without fully-operational security functions and self-protections.

The service should also be designed and implemented to transition to a fallback state if it detects that any of the external mechanisms it relies on to accomplish its security functions (e.g., SAML Attribute Authority, PKI components) become unavailable.

The following approaches to the design, implementation, and sustainment (operation and maintenance) of the Web service will increase its ability to recognize, resist, and recover from DoS:

- Design to include redundancy of critical functions, with diversity of how those critical functions are implemented.
- Design exception and error handling capabilities that:
  - Are specific to the various types of faults expected (do not simply throw general exceptions for every fault)
  - Detect, recognize, and respond specifically and appropriately to attack patterns associated with denial of service

  - Always fail into a secure state
  - Gracefully degrade performance or perform partial shutdown of functions (but not security- or protection-related functions) according to a predefined plan
  - Are configurable by the administrator at runtime
  - Perform transaction rollback and checkpoint restart (for Web services that update data stores)
  - Perform informative event logging
  - Generate only *safe* error messages to users (i.e., error messages that do not contain information that can be exploited by an attacker to craft a more effective attack).
- Use defensive programming techniques and information hiding to make the Web service software more robust.
- Through QoS and reliable messaging, Web services can ensure that messages are not lost even if the network is saturated.

Web services, due to either their implementation or that of the frameworks on which they depend, may begin to degrade through residual cache data, temporary files, or even a fragmented hard drive. To prevent availability risks due to this degradation, it is useful to perform periodic software rejuvenations and reconfigurations to return the service software to a known reliable state.[51] The techniques used vary among OSs and applications. Rejuvenation is common in organizations taking advantage of virtualization, because it can be performed by taking virtual machine *snapshots* and reverting back to them after a period of time.

Organizations deploying and implementing Web services should also be aware of two of the most common accidental threats against availability: service recursion and service deadlock. Through Web services' support for dynamic discovery and binding, it is possible that a single Web service may attempt to bind to itself, possibly resulting in a DoS. Deadlocks are an equally important threat that arises when multiple entities are requesting access to the same resource.

3.8.1 Failover

One of the primary goals of a distributed system is the ability to recover when a node in the system fails. Through dynamic discovery and binding, Web services can be designed to recover if a single service fails, whether the failure is accidental or intentional. UDDI supports listing multiple URIs for each Web service. When one instance of a Web service has failed, requesters can use an alternate URI.

Using UDDI to support failover causes the UDDI registry to become a single point of failure. To remedy this, UDDI supports replication. Through replication, UDDI registries can support multiple nodes, where each node is an instance of the UDDI registry. This way, backup nodes can be used when an individual node is faced with a DoS attack.

3.8.2 Quality of Service

Most Web services deployed do not provide guarantees for QoS. QoS defines what the expected level of performance a particular Web service will have. By prioritizing traffic, overall performance of the system

[51] Software rejuvenation was first proposed by Y. Huang, C. Kintala, N. Kolettis, and N. D. Fulton in *Software Rejuvenation: Analysis, Module and Applications*, in Proc. of 25th Symposium on Fault Tolerant Computing, FTCS-25, pages 381–390, Pasadena, California, June 1995.

can be improved, allowing the system to make informed decisions when faced with few resources. For example, a Web service operating on a saturated network may use prioritization to allow only the highest priority traffic to be processed while letting the other traffic wait until network traffic returns to normal.

Standards are beginning to be developed and released to support availability of Web services. In particular, two competing standards are available that provide reliable messaging support: WS-Reliability and WS-ReliableMessaging, discussed in Section 3.8.3. Standards and techniques for providing QoS, detecting, resisting and recovering from DoS attacks are still under development. Sections 3.8.4 and 3.8.5 discuss two common design or implementation defects that can lead to a loss of availability without the malicious intent: deadlock and recursion.

The standards state that other QoS parameters, such as rate of failure or average latency, are out of scope because they are usually dealt with by lower layer protocols. For Web services to truly support QoS, existing QoS support must be extended so that the packets corresponding to individual Web service messages can be routed accordingly.

3.8.3 Reliable Messaging

The WS-Reliability and WS-ReliableMessaging standards provide guaranteed message delivery using one of the following semantics:

- At-Least-Once semantics, which is a guarantee that a message will be delivered.
- At-Most-Once semantics, which is a guarantee that a duplicate message will not be delivered.
- Exactly-Once semantics, which is a guarantee that a message will be delivered without duplication.

In addition to the message guarantee semantics, both standards provide a mechanism for sending messages in order. These features are crucial for critical applications that may rely on Web services. Previously, implementers would have to develop their own reliability mechanisms, which could prove costly or ineffective in practice. With the advent of these standards, robust implementations can be developed and used in the development of reliable Web services. Nevertheless, the existence of two competing standards makes it difficult for organizations to fully adopt either standard.

3.8.4 Handling Service Deadlock

Deadlock is a condition that occurs when two processes are each waiting for the other to complete before proceeding. The result is that neither process can continue. Deadlocks can occur whenever the following four conditions are present in a system:

- Mutual exclusion. A resource can only be accessed by one process at a time.
- Hold and wait. Processes already holding resources can request more resources.
- No preemption. Only the process holding a resource has the power to release it.
- Circular wait. Processes form a circular chain of waiting.

Ideally, either the programs that experience deadlock or the underlying operating system would be able to automatically detect and recover from the deadlock, but it is difficult for individual systems in a SOA to detect deadlocked SOAP requests. SOA environments are susceptible to both local and distributed deadlocks. In a local deadlock, a provider is poorly designed and has an internal deadlock preventing it from returning a response to the requester. In a distributed deadlock, one Web service that is not responding may lead to the entire choreography stalling until an administrator notices.

If deadlock occurs, multiple requesters could have their requests blocked indefinitely and could cause the clients awaiting the responses to suspend all other activities until the responses are received, thus rendering them unavailable to their users. Because Web services can be sequenced (i.e., a provider responding to one requester sometimes needing to act as a requester of services from another provider), the probabilities of a circular chain of waiting are increased. A deadlock may also occur if one of the systems in a circular chain of waiting crashes during a request, leaving some systems endlessly waiting for a response.

3.8.5 Service Recursion

Similar to a deadlock, Web services can also experience an infinite recursion, where Web services keep initiating requests to one another to solve a problem. For example, Web service A implements a service by forwarding it to Web service B, and Web service B searches the UDDI registry to dynamically bind a Web service that performs the required functionality and finds Web service A, so it forwards the request back to Web service A. Because neither Web service implements the required functionality, they will continue to send requests until they run out of resources. Such a situation needs to be carefully avoided, which may be difficult in a highly dynamic SOA.

Execution flow diagrams are the method development teams usually use to mitigate deadlock and recursion. These diagrams are fairly effective for predicting interactions within a single application. The interfaces from the Web service under development with other services, especially those provided by third parties (COTS, Open Source Software [OSS]), are more difficult to manage.

At the design level, service interface information for third-party services needs to be thoroughly reviewed so shortcomings can be effectively mitigated in the Web service design. At the design level, the most effective antideadlock mechanisms are to implement asynchronous (non-blocking) service-to-service calls and to design the Web service to use message buffering.

3.9 Securing the Discovery Service: Secure Interfaces to UDDI and WSDL

UDDI provides a medium for publishing and locating Web services. Originally, UDDI's main focus was the Universal Business Registry (UBR), a publicly accessible directory of Web services. Most Web services are not for public use, so the UDDI specification expanded to include private implementations of the UDDI registry. A private UDDI registry provides a mechanism for internal applications and users to discover and access Web services within an organization with little, if any, human interaction. UDDI v3 was approved as an OASIS Standard in 2005, but as of this writing a number of UDDI registries implement UDDI v2, so UDDI v2 is also discussed. The following subsections provide additional details into the structure, operations, and security inherent to UDDI, as well as explanations of the APIs relevant to UDDI.

3.9.1 UDDI Structure

UDDI registries provide information about organizations and the Web services they provide through three different interfaces:

- White pages, which provide the identity and contact information of an organization
- Yellow pages, which divide organizations into categories and provide information about their services

- Green pages, which provide information about an organization's services: the locations of services, and binding information.

There are six data types in a UDDI registry that provide all the information:

- **businessEntity**. Holds the name, address, and contact information of an organization
- **businessService**. Holds technical data about what services and products the organization offers
- **bindingTemplate**. Provides details on a particular Web service offered
- **tModel**. Defines how to interact with the target Web service, which is usually done by providing a technical specification, such as a wire protocol, interchange format, or interchange sequencing rule (e.g., WSDL document)
- **publisherAssertion**. Describes the relationship between businessEntity entries
- **subscription**. Describes a request to monitor changes to certain entities within the registry.

A WSDL document provides requesters with all the necessary information to send SOAP requests to a provider service. A WSDL document defines services as a collection of endpoints, which are referred to as ports. It also provides an abstract description of the types of messages and operations a Web service performs along with what inputs are required for each operation and as what format the result is returned. A UDDI registry provides a method to search for Web services and provides requester services with the location of the WSDL document for the target Web service.

UDDI registries are generally hosted within organizational boundaries and allow access to certain services within an individual SOA to be restricted. There are four types of private registries:

- **Internet-based services registry**. Hosted by a group of organizations and provides information about these organizations for public consumption
- **Portal registry**. Resides outside of an organization's firewall and provides information about that particular organization's Web services
- **Partner catalog registry**. Resides on an internal network and provides information on the services offered by a particular organization and its partners
- **Internal services registry**. Resides on an internal network and provides information on the services offered within that network.

In addition, UDDI v3 provides a framework for access privileges to keep portions of the registry available only to authorized users.

3.9.2 UDDI Operations

In UDDI, the process of locating Web services through a registry is referred to as *discovery*. There are two types of discovery: direct discovery and indirect discovery. In direct discovery, the information is retrieved through a registry maintained by the service provider. In indirect discovery, the information is retrieved through a third party registry.

UDDI provides three SOAP-based APIs to access the registry:

- A publishing API is used to place information into the registry. The publishing is restricted, so publishers must be authenticated. Authentication can be performed using a username/password combination, SAML, Kerberos, or some other method.
- An inquiry API provides read-only access to the registry. The inquiry API allows Web services to search for organization details, services offered, and binding information for the services. This API is usually publicly accessible. In UDDI v2, the inquiry API does not support authentication, but in UDDI v3, authentication can be required for inquiries—limiting access to the registry only to trusted Web services.
- UDDI v3 introduces a new subscription API that provides notifications about additions or updates to the registry. The subscription API is also restricted, requiring authentication by the registry.

In addition to the SOAP-based APIs, many implementations of UDDI registries provide a Web interface for publishing to and searching the registry. Because this is not part of the UDDI standard and is not implemented by all UDDI registry vendors, these UDDI Web interfaces are not covered in this guide.

3.9.3 Secure Access to the Registry

As described in Section 3.9.2, some portions of the UDDI API require authentication. SOAP over HTTPS is usually required to make certain that publisher credentials cannot be intercepted during transmission. In addition, all publishers should be designated as Tier 1 publishers. In UDDI v2, Tier 1 publishers have defined restrictions for what services they can publish to the registry. In a private registry, these restrictions can vary based on the needs of the organization. In contrast, the specification does not require restrictions on a Tier 2 publisher.

Some UDDI registries provide the ability to restrict publishers' activities at the account level, which provides some control over Tier 2 publishers. UDDI v3 provides the ability to define policies, which provide finer control over publishers than the Tier model available in v2. UDDI v3 adds support for XML Signatures to the registry, providing a way for inquirers to verify the integrity and publisher of data in the registry. In UDDI registries, a publisher is only allowed to alter entries the publisher created, so inquirers can be reasonably certain that any changes made to an entry in the registry were made by the appropriate publisher. Nevertheless, even with digital signatures, there is no guarantee the information in a UDDI registry is correct—only that it was published by a trusted entity.

3.9.4 Service Inquiry API

The inquiry API is used to search for Web services within the UDDI registry that meet the requester's needs. In UDDI v2, the inquiry API is accessed through SOAP over HTTP and requires no authentication. The requester must have a pre-existing trust relationship with the UDDI service, which can be achieved by accessing a private UDDI registry within the organization or a trusted public UDDI registry (e.g., the UBR). Most UDDI registries run from a functioning Web server and are unaware as to whether or not the Web server is using HTTPS. It may be possible to configure a UDDI v2 registry's inquiry API to use SSL/TLS, which in turn can be configured for authentication in addition to encryption.

UDDI v3 specifies that the inquiry API can be accessed over HTTPS and supports authorization. If a UDDI v3 service is being used with authentication, the requester has previously established a relationship with the registry and can likely trust its results. In UDDI v3, authentication usually consists of a username and plaintext password transmitted over SSL/TLS, but the UDDI specification states that any authentication method can be used to access the registry, from X.509 certificates to SAML assertions. Also, because UDDI v3 allows the inquiry API to use SSL/TLS, the requesting service can be certain that the results from the registry were not tampered with during transit.

In UDDI v2, there is no way for the requester to verify the integrity or origin of data retrieved through the registry. Some integrity assumptions may be made because publishers are required to authenticate to the registry, but it is not possible to determine whether or not a particular publisher is legitimate.

In UDDI v3, all data entries stored in the registry can be signed using XML Signatures. After receiving information about a candidate, the requester can retrieve the public key associated with the candidate and verify the integrity of the data from the registry. This is the best solution for verifying that entries in a UDDI registry are valid.

In UDDI v2, it is possible to include digital signatures for entries in the optional "description" element of each data type, as this element is designed to contain textual information about the entry. Both the requester and the publisher must agree on a protocol for performing this type of signature so that verification can be possible.

3.9.5 Service Publishing API

The publishing API is used to publish information about a Web service in the UDDI registry. According to the UDDI specification, SOAP over HTTPS should be used exclusively for all calls in the publisher API. In addition, the publisher must authenticate with the UDDI registry via the "get_authToken" call. All calls within the publisher API require the authentication token to be passed as an argument.

The UDDI specification does not define what authentication methods should be used, so they can range from a simple username/password combination to a SAML assertion, depending on the implementation. Once the publisher has received the authorization token, it must be kept securely until it is has been discarded so that an attacker cannot use the token.

In a UDDI registry, there are limits for how much each publisher can publish. In UDDI v2, the limits are broken up between Tier 1 publishers and Tier 2 publishers. Tier 1 publishers are limited to publishing a hard-coded number of UDDI entries.[52] Tier 2 publishers have no hard-coded limit and they are to be strictly monitored by the UDDI registry's operator. In UDDI v3, operators have more fine-grained control over the limits imposed upon publishers through policies.

A requester can independently verify the validity of these structures using the UDDI API. In UDDI v3, an additional method for verifying the publisher of any data structure is an XML Signature. When using a UDDI v3 registry, XML Signatures should be used, as they are the best method for verification. If signatures are to be used in a UDDI v2 registry, it may be possible to place them in the description element. The publisher and the inquirer must have a predefined method for calculating signatures in this case.

Publisher assertions are used to establish a relationship between two businessEntities, such as one entity being a subsidiary of the other. For a publisherAssertion to be recognized by the UDDI registry, both entities must create the publisherAssertion. This allows inquirers to be certain that there is a relationship between two entities.

The publisher is also responsible for verifying that the records and assertions published are correct. Any mistake made while publishing will result in incorrect results when inquirers access the UDDI registry.

---

[52] The UDDI v2 Tier 1 publishing limits are outlined in the specification, available at http://uddi.org/pubs/ProgrammersAPI-V2.04-Published-20020719.pdf.

3.9.6 UDDI and WSDL

While UDDI provides a registry for searching for and automatically connecting to Web services, there is no mechanism for describing how to connect to candidate services. This is done through the WSDL document. A Web service's WSDL document is referenced through the bindingTemplate and tModel data structures.[53]

When publishing a Web service, a UDDI publisher must make certain that there is a tModel associated with the WSDL for the Web service being published. These are referred to as wsdlSpec tModels. wsdlSpec tModels allow inquirers to locate Web services that correspond to the same published WSDL document. For example, there are standard WSDL specifications for UDDI and NCES services, but there may be multiple Web services that implement them.

tModels are referenced from the bindingTemplate data structure by providing a tModelInstanceInfo entry for each tModel that corresponds to the service's WSDL document. A tModel provides the location to a Web service's WSDL document, but the bindingTemplate's accessPoint element specifies the location of the Web service itself. UDDI allows for Web services and WSDL documents to be in separate locations.

Once the requester receives the WSDL document for the candidate Web service, it must be validated. The simplest method for doing this is to provide a digital signature of the WSDL document for the requester to use. WSDL v1.1 does not provide an internal mechanism for signing WSDL documents. Until such a mechanism is available, the candidate Web service should provide an external signature for the WSDL document or the requester should independently verify via out-of-band communications that the site providing the WSDL document is a trusted entity.

Requesters cannot connect to most providers without some form of authentication. WSDL v1.1 does not provide a method for specifying the security requirements of a Web service. Future versions of WSDL are slated to have this feature. At the moment, the requesting Web service must use some external method for determining what authentication requirements a candidate service has. This can be done using tModels.

In a UDDI registry, a bindingTemplate structure can hold zero or more references to tModels. tModels are used to represent the different WSDL service interfaces, but may be used to reference other metadata related to the Web service.

Because tModels are used to describe the particular interfaces and behavior of a Web service, an additional unique tModel could be developed for each method of authentication that Web services in the registry may use. When a requesting Web service sees this tModel, the requester will know what methods of authentication the candidate Web service requires. This approach is implemented for the NCES service discovery services.

3.10 Summary

Web service security standards are developed and maintained by several different organizations: W3C, OASIS, Liberty Alliance, and an industry forum headed by Microsoft and IBM. Some industry forum specifications, such as WS-Security, are submitted to OASIS for maintenance and acceptance as a standard. In contrast, other industry forum specifications directly conflict with OASIS or W3C standards, like the WS-Reliability and WS-ReliableMessaging standards. Where such conflicts exist, one or more of

53 This document provides only an overview of how the WSDL is entered into a UDDI registry. For a more detailed explanation, see *Using WSDL in a UDDI Registry,* available at http://www.oasis-open.org/committees/uddi-spec/doc/tn/uddi-spec-tc-tn-wsdl-v202-20040631.htm.

the involved standards may change or cease to be implemented. Organizations should take care when adopting such overlapping standards to avoid expensive upgrades or overhauls of the SOA.

The WS-Security specification provides confidentiality, integrity, and non-repudiation using the XML Signature and XML Encryption standards. It also supports authentication via SAML, X.509, Kerberos, REL, and username and password combinations. WS-Security should be employed as an integral part of any organization's Web services deployment, but it does not secure the entire SOA. For Web services that were not implemented with support for WS-Security, XML gateways can be used to act as intermediaries and apply WS-Security to SOAP requests and verify SOAP responses, using HTTPS to secure communication directly between the legacy Web service and the XML gateway. While confidentiality and integrity can be assured via WS-Security, there are no established standards for specifying the required QoP of a particular SOAP message or Web service. By sharing the QoP information about individual Web services, requesters and providers can support dynamic binding in a secure environment.

WS-Security provides a powerful framework for authentication within a single organization. For authentication within large organizations or across multiple organizations, using a single TTP may not be feasible. To facilitate authentication across trust boundaries, a trust federation framework should be adopted. Organizations face several options: Liberty Alliance, WS-Federation, and Shibboleth. Liberty Alliance works closely with OASIS, and SAML v2.0 incorporated many of the features from earlier Liberty Alliance specifications. Because the same functionality is provided by each framework, the choice may largely depend on whether COTS products already deployed support one of these frameworks.

Distributed authorization is becoming increasingly common in organizational SOAs where each Web service is a PEP that communicates with a PDP to get authorization information. To this end, SAML and XACML were developed to provide support for multiple authorization models. SAML assertions are generated by TTPs and can be used as security tokens by entities within the SOA. When a request is received, PEPs use the SAML protocol to communicate with the PDP to determine whether the requester is authorized. XACML provides a flexible, extensible policy language and mechanisms for querying XACML policies. Similarly, authorization rules may affect individual content or services. Security metadata can be used to determine what entities are authorized to access content or services. By providing policy along with the content or service, PEPs are able to make some authorization decisions without communicating remotely over the network.

Securing the discovery process is also important for an organizational SOA. If the registry can be corrupted, or if the provider's WSDL document is wrong, an attacker may gain access to restricted information or the entire SOA may fail. UDDI v3 provides support for digitally signing registry information using XML Signatures, allowing requesters to verify the authenticity and the integrity of the information. WSDL documents, however, do not inherently support digital signatures, meaning that verifying the authenticity and integrity requires an out-of-band mechanism. True automated discovery is still hampered by the fact that even though an individual's identity is trusted, the published service may be malicious or may itself use a malicious service.

Some of the biggest challenges facing Web services are in the realm of accountability and availability. While XML Signatures and the algorithms defined in FIPS 186-2 can be used to support non-repudiation, accountability also requires the use of auditing. There is no standard for distributed auditing within a Web services environment. NIST SP 800-92, *Guide to Security Log Management*[54] provides guidance on

[54] NIST SP 800-92, *Guide to Security Log Management*, is available at http://csrc.nist.gov/publications/nistpubs/.

managing security logs within an organization, but any portion of a SOA transaction outside of the organization's control may not retain security logs.

Availability is increasingly becoming a concern with Web services, so QoS is becoming increasingly important. For mission critical applications to be built with the SOA paradigm, the SOA must be able to withstand one or more services becoming unavailable, either due to a DoS or a failure. Web services' support for dynamic discovery and binding allows for failover Web services to be accessed when a DoS occurs. Similarly, reliable messaging technologies can be used to ensure that messages will be received in spite of a DoS attack. Finally, QoS technologies can be used to prioritize Web service traffic so that high priority Web services will still remain functional in the face of an attack on the availability of the network.

4. Human User's Entry Point into the SOA: Web Portals

A *Web portal* is a starting point for Web activities. By logging into a Web portal, a user is granted access to the information and services connected to the authenticating portal. Common implementations for portals are Internet search engines that expand into information centers, and Web interfaces for corporate knowledge management systems.

Web portals that sit at the boundary of a SOA have multiple roles: a Web server for users and a requester to other Web services in the SOA. This dual role brings with it security implications that could impact Web services interacting with the portal. Some of these implications include:

- **Authentication.** Who is sending this message?
- **Authorization.** Is the authenticated subject entitled to access?
- **Audit.** Can it be proved that this transaction occurred?
- **Integrity.** Was the message, or the system, tampered with?
- **Confidentiality.** Can the information be read while it is in transit? In storage?
- **Privacy.** Can personally identifiable information be released to the public?
- **Availability.** Is it vulnerable to a denial of service attack (brute force or otherwise)?
- **Non-Repudiation.** Can it be proven that the sender and the recipient did in fact send and receive the message?
- **Policy Administration.** How easy is it to apply or change a security policy rule or configuration parameter?

Additionally, Web service faces many challenges to fulfilling these basic security requirements. The threats to Web services security include both the traditional exploits associated with the underlying protocols such as HTTP, as well as new threats associated with new protocols and services, such as SOAP and XML.

This section expands on the information provided above, with particular focus on explaining the role of proxy agents, authorization and access control considerations for portals, and potential mechanisms for enforcing XML filtering constraints on content provided to portal users.

4.1 Proxy Agents

As mentioned above, Web services that reside on the edge of the SOA are used to represent users during communications from the client on the edge of the service and other Web services. A number of Web service invocations are at the request of users through edge applications, such as portals, Web servers, and single sign-on servers. These edge applications are server-based Web applications that interface, as proxy agents on behalf of the user, with the Web services in the SOA. All security functions that require direct interaction with users (via their clients) are expected to be performed by the edge applications. The Web services connected to the portal would then presume that when the edge applications assert a user's authenticity and privileges, such an assertion is trustworthy.

For Web services to communicate, the interacting parties must trust each other. When communicating using Web services, there are a number of different entities involved: the client application through which the user operates, a portal, a requester, a provider service, an SSO server, and SAML-enabled Web applications.

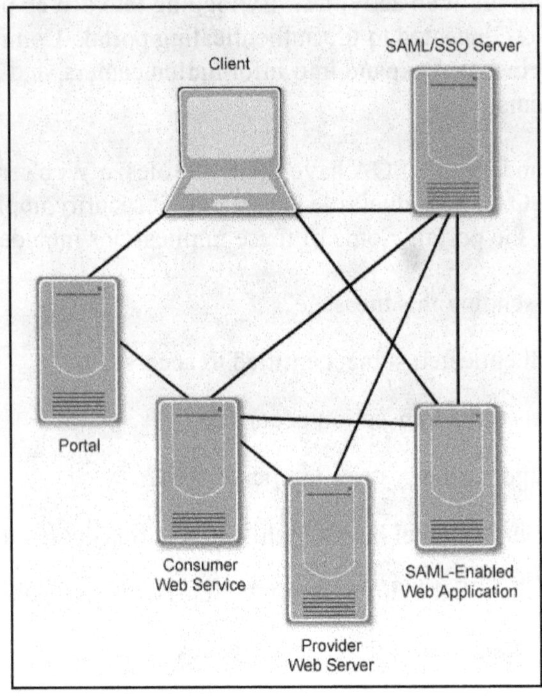

Figure 4-1. Web Services Trust Relationships

In a Web services trust environment, a user will communicate with an SSO server and one or more SAML-enabled Web applications, as shown in Figure 4-1. For this SSO environment to function correctly, all three entities must trust each other. A user may also access a portal application, which provides Web service proxy agents access to providers on behalf of the user. In addition, requesters will often talk to providers on their own behalf. For all of these interactions to function, the entities involved must trust one another. WS-Security enables two Web services to trust each other, while SAML enables one entity to assert that it trusts another entity. In this type of configuration, it is possible to build a chain of trust, where a Web service trusts another Web service regardless of the fact the two Web services have no direct relationship.

4.2 Using the Portal to Control User Authorization and Access to Web Services

A portal may use SAML assertions to express a user's identity to other Web services, so SAML assertions may be extended into authorization and access controls. Portals can be implemented using one of the available Liberty or SAML libraries or using one of the many COTS products that will act as an identity server. By implementing an identity server, the portal's presentation functions are combined with the SSO and distributed access management services, providing only authorized information to be presented to the user.

COTS identity servers provide robust support for the complexities of the SAML specification. Additionally, most COTS identity providers support a wide variety of authentication mechanisms—from certificates to passwords. While these are designed to prevent attacks at the protocol level, COTS identity providers must be configured correctly to be secure.

4.3 Portal Interaction with the SOA's Discovery Service

As described in Section 4.2, pages presented to the user can be tailored to analyze a user's credentials to prevent users from searching for services that the user is not authorized to interact with.

If a portal's SAML assertion (on behalf of a user) does not include the proper credentials to access a service (as determined by the discovery service), the user will not be permitted to know that the service exists. Controlling access to services at the discovery level may be beneficial to the service. It can simplify the administration of access controls required to maintain the service's expected level of security.

4.4 Summary

In a SOA, the Web portal is an SSO starting point for users interfacing with a SOA. Web portals interact with provider services and identity providers to perform actions on behalf of the user. By acting as a middleman between the user and the provider services, portals must provide authentication information about the user, coordinate with the provider's authorization mechanisms and policy administration as well as provide auditing services, integrity, confidentiality, availability, and non-repudiation of messages sent to both the user and provider. Through SAML and WS-Security, these goals can be achieved. SAML allows the user to authenticate with the identity provider and will provide SAML assertions that can be sent along with all requests on behalf of the user. Provider services can then verify the contents of the SAML assertions and determine whether the user is authorized to perform the action.

5. Secure Web Service-Enabling of Legacy Applications

Migrating applications to Web services can expose the legacy application and backend databases to new threats that were not considered when the applications were initially developed. Securely enabling Web services on legacy applications requires customized Web service adapters to be securely coded and implemented. Like any Web service, these adapters must be resistant to attack. Authentication, authorization and access control are among the first concerns to address when migrating a legacy application to a Web service architecture.

5.1 Legacy Authentication to Web Services

Web applications are typically designed for client-server communication. SSL/TLS allows both the client and server to authenticate their PKI certificates, yet in most situations, Web servers are not configured to authenticate clients' SSL/TLS certificates. Instead, they rely on less strong authentication, such as a username and password. Authenticating both the client and server certificates can allow for strong authentication between Web services. Authentication using Web service technologies can be achieved using WS-Security as described in Section 3.1.2.

To Web service-enable a standalone legacy application using its own proprietary authentication mechanism requires some mechanism for mapping Web service credentials to their associated legacy credentials and an adapter for mapping incoming or outgoing Web service messages to the legacy application's protocols. Typically, these credentials are in the form of a username and password combination; in some cases, these are stored or transmitted via an insecure encryption scheme. The legacy adapter should encrypt and securely store the legacy credentials when they are not in use. In addition, the adapter connection to the legacy application should be secured using technologies like SSL/TLS or IPsec.

Whenever possible, legacy adapters should not be developed from scratch. A robust, well-tested third-party product is likely to be more secure and reliable than a from-scratch adapter. There are a number of COTS products (e.g., middleware solutions) capable of integrating with legacy applications.

Regardless of how the Web service-to-legacy adapter is implemented, it should include logging sufficient to satisfy the audit and reporting requirements discussed in Section 5.5. Ideally, the Web service and legacy application should support a single authentication method throughout the end-to-end solution.

5.2 Authorization and Access Control in Legacy Applications

If the legacy Web application performs its own user authorizations (rather than relying on a centralized authorization service provided by a portal or SSO server), the application process that allocates permissions and privileges to users and processes must be correct and unable to be subverted. The authorization process will have to trust the authentication system's assurance that the users and processes to be authorized have already been properly authenticated.

If the authorization information used by the application will be stored and managed in a directory (for example, the LDAP or X.500 directory used by the PKI), the transmission path over which authorization information will be sent from the directory to the application's authorization process should be secured. When the authorization data is stored in the directory, it should be protected by the directory's access controls and, when feasible, by encryption.

If standard user/group/world authorizations are inadequately fine-grained, the application's authorization system may have to implement its own access control mechanism (Section 3.5.1 discusses access control models).

Because of the additional requirements for access control for systems that contain or process sensitive information, it may be necessary for such applications to augment the underlying file system's access controls by ensuring that the data that require additional protection are encrypted when they are written by the application to a file system directory (or database). In practical terms, encryption of data at rest is a form of access control: access to the encrypted data is controlled by limiting access to the cryptographic keys required to decrypt that data.

The application's design should implement separation of duties, roles and privileges for subjects as well as minimize the resources needed by the application process. When designing the application, the actions that any component will be allowed to perform should be explicitly specified. Custom processes and scripts should not be granted or allowed to retain privileges that would enable them to perform actions not expressly defined for them. Instead, each process in the application should be designed to do the following:

- Perform only the actions explicitly defined
- Strictly enforce the processing order defined
- Call only those other processes and libraries absolutely needed to invoke
- Execute only one task at a time
- Initiate a new task only after the previous task has completed
- Access only data absolutely needed to successfully perform tasks.

5.3 Extending Non-Web Applications to Be Able to Participate in SOAs

Allowing non-Web applications such as database and directory server applications to securely interact with Web services involves many of the same measures as enabling Web applications. The same procedures are used for creating a Web service and extending an existing application's functionality as a discoverable Web service.

Web services can extend any application, as long as there are robust and easy-to-use business objects or an API built into the application. It will be more difficult to Web service-enable applications that have business logic built into the graphical user interface (GUI), because the business logic must usually be rewritten to accommodate the new Web service extension of the business object.

5.4 Public Key Enabling Concerns Specific to Web Services and SOAs

Both SSL/TLS and WS-Security, the primary methods for securing SOAP messages, rely on PKI certificates for authentication. Many legacy applications only support username and password authentication over time. Organizations may benefit from transitioning these legacy applications to PKI authentication. Initially, the legacy application should provide the capability for users to test their certificates while maintaining username password access. Then, the application should allow users who have certificates to authenticate using these certificates while still allowing users to authenticate with their existing usernames and passwords. Once users have become familiar with certificate-based authentication, the application should publish a date after which usernames and passwords will no longer be accepted. In the transition to Web services, an API should be developed that can be used to communicate with the discovery service as well as authenticate users.

For applications with a large number of current users, an applet can be written to establish a mapping between an existing username—and associated privileges—and a subscriber certificate. The first time each user is authenticated based on the certificate, the user will be asked to provide the old username and password. The applet will then establish the mapping of the privileges associated with that username to the new certificate, so that the next time the user logs in, those privileges will be granted based on the certificate presented, without the user being required to enter the old username and password.[55]

5.5 Accountability for Legacy Application Transactions

In accordance with the security functions provided by authorization and access control measures, sound Web services security practices also include the maintenance of auditing records. Auditing should be done to maintain appropriate accountability for legacy application transactions in the Web services environment.

The legacy application's auditing mechanisms should be developed to provide sufficient information and secure storage for audit data. Verbose logging is beneficial to later analysis of the system. Appropriate review procedures can identify anomalous access control situations, which may indicate an attacker's presence. To support analysis, logs should be stored securely for an appropriate length of time, which is usually determined by the organizational policies. NIST SP 800-92 provides guidance for managing logs within an organization.

5.6 Database Security Challenges in SOA Environments

When a database application is exposed as a service or is simply accessed by a Web service, the security of the database relies entirely on the security of the applications directly accessing it. The exposing application should account for confirming the requester's authorization to access the database. Additionally, the application must filter requests before forwarding them on to the database. Incoming requests may include SQL injection attacks or other attempts to subvert the database or retrieve sensitive information. The application must also filter the data before providing it to the requester to prevent unintentional leakage.

5.7 Maintaining Security of Legacy Systems Exposed via Web Services

When integrating legacy systems as backend servers in a SOA, developers must make sure that security does not stop at the connection between the SOA and the Web service interface to the legacy system. Instead, the developer should incorporate the following measures to ensure the integrity of the data being processed:

- Establish end-to-end user authentication. Set up an end-to-end user authentication mechanism that reaches from requesters to the mainframe or other backend legacy server.
- Establish an end-to-end encrypted data channel. Use encryption from the individual requesters to the Web service interface and from the Web service interface to the legacy backend system. This is done to ensure that sensitive data are not exposed in transit over external and internal networks. If the

[55] For further guidance on public key implementation, see NIST SP 800-32, *Introduction to Public Key Technology and the Federal PKI Infrastructure* and NIST SP 800-44, *Guidelines on Securing Public Web Servers,* available at http://csrc.nist.gov/publications/nistpubs/.

backend system does not natively support encrypted data channels, IPsec or SSL tunneling software can provide an encrypted data channel.

- Implement public key security end-to-end. Deploy public key components all the way from the requester to the backend system and integrate them with existing security systems.

In addition to certificate-based identification and authentication (I&A), the Web service will also need to perform application-level monitoring and auditing of Web connections, access events, and security violations.

In certain high-risk environments, a second factor of authentication, in addition to PKI certificate-based I&A, may be desired. This second factor may include a static password, a dynamic password, or a biometric. In some applications, the user's initial authentication may be via a second-factor mechanism during the authenticated session.

Security for the mainframe was not designed with the SOA processing model in mind. Rather, mainframe security was designed for a closed, well-defined, and tightly controlled environment. Key characteristics of such environments include a known and relatively trusted user population, a well-defined set of applications, and firm connectivity boundaries. Application developers need to leverage existing backend mainframe security systems.

5.8 Summary

Secure Web service-enabling of legacy applications allows new SOA applications to leverage the functionality and services provided by an organization's legacy systems. This can prove to be cost-effective when developing Web services that require legacy functionality. Web service-enabling legacy applications can introduce Web service threats to the legacy application and provide a new avenue of attack into the legacy application. Legacy applications built without understanding of SOA or networking may lead to the discovery of new vulnerabilities in the application. When Web service-enabling a legacy application, it is important to be aware of these threats and use appropriate technologies to mitigate them. Similarly, the mechanisms used to Web service-enable legacy software must also be secure, to prevent introducing new vulnerabilities into the system.

Ideally, legacy applications should be modified to support Web service standards, but this may not always be possible. If the application was originally designed as a Web application, it can be configured to use SSL/TLS for authentication, confidentiality and integrity between the Web service front-end and the application itself. In addition, many legacy applications have built-in authentication and authorization mechanisms. If possible, these should be upgraded to support SOA technologies; otherwise the Web service front-end will have to map SOA identities and permissions to those used by the legacy application. While it is important to provide an updated authentication and authorization mechanism, it is equally important to take advantage of logging facilities provided by the application. In addition, these logs should be integrated into the system-wide log management infrastructure. By exposing legacy functionality as a Web service, there are a number of potential attacks that may surface, requiring the Web service front-end to be carefully designed, implemented, and deployed to take full advantage of the legacy application's security functionality while providing the security needed to protect against threats introduced by the SOA.

6. Secure Implementation Tools and Technologies

When implementing a secure Web service, developers should be aware of how to use the available development tools, techniques, and languages in a secure manner, in addition to implementing the security functionality already discussed in this guide. While security functionality is an important aspect of secure Web services, security functionality can be compromised by poorly implemented software. See Appendix A for a discussion of some attacks to which Web services are susceptible. The following sections outline the various developer toolkits, XML parsers, available development languages, and security testing methodologies that can aid in testing a Web service.

6.1 Web Services Developer Toolkits

When choosing an appropriate Web services developer toolkit, it is important to first determine whether there are any language requirements of the Web service. Should it be able to interact with a .NET environment, a Java environment, or natively compiled libraries? In most cases, either a Java or .NET Web service will be able to meet all of the functional requirements of the system, but there are times when a Web service written using C or C++ may be necessary. If the language requirement is not an obstacle, there are further attributes of a Web service development toolkit to consider.

The most important aspect of a Web service development toolkit is its ability to interoperate with Web services developed using other toolkits. The SOAP and WSDL specifications developed by W3C left some design choices to individual Web service toolkit developers, making Web services less interoperable. In particular, by default Java and .NET Web services may not be able to communicate with one another. To this end, WS-I developed WS-I Basic Profile 1.1, which specifies exactly how the WSDL and SOAP specifications should be implemented to achieve full interoperability. Toolkits that support WS-I Basic Profile 1.1 will be able to interoperate with Web services from other toolkits with—at most—only minor changes to the Web service being developed.[56]

Additionally, WS-I is working on WS-I Basic Security Profile 1.0, which will allow Web services to implement interoperable authentication mechanisms. WS-Security implementations do not always interoperate well with other Web services, so the WS-I Basic Security Profile will aid in developing secure interoperable Web services. As this specification has not yet been ratified, few (if any) Web service toolkits support it. Until the WS-I Basic Security Profile has been released by WS-I, toolkits should be used that provide support for (or have libraries available for) the WS-Security and SAML specifications, which are the most commonly used tools for securing and authenticating Web services.

Finally, WS toolkits should ease the burden placed on the Web service developer by providing tools that will create *stubs*, the Web service-specific code, that the developer can use without having to delve into XML or SOAP specifics. Usually, these tools are in the form of a command-line program that will take either a pre-existing application and develop the WSDL or develop stubs from a pre-existing WSDL.

6.2 XML Parsers

XML parsers are the first portion of a Web service that process input from other Web services. A poorly designed or poorly configured XML parser can be used to compromise the Web service regardless of how secure the Web service is. To this end, it is important to use robust and proven XML parsers.

[56] DoD has created the Federated Development and Certification Environment (FDCE), which provides the policies, processes, and infrastructure to allow services to be progressively refined, tested, evaluated, and certified in increasingly rigorous situation leading to an operational deployment. Web services certified by FDCE will have some level of assurance that they will be fully interoperable with other FDCE-certified Web services. Similar efforts are being proposed by other organizations within the commercial and Federal spaces.

An improperly configured XML Parser is susceptible to several attacks:

- Large or recursive XML documents can overload the XML parser and lead to a DoS.
- XML documents can be configured to refer to and use local files. This can lead to an attacker gaining knowledge about the local system.
- External references to other XML documents or XML schemas can be used to bypass XML validators.

All of these XML parser security concerns can be overcome by properly configuring the system. In particular, oversized XML documents can be prevented by configuring the Web server on which the Web service is running to only accept messages up to a certain size. When the oversized XML document is passed to the Web server, it will prevent the entire document from reaching the Web service. The other XML attacks can be prevented by developing robust local XML schemas for the Web service and configuring the XML parser to validate all incoming XML traffic against the local schemas rather than against remote schemas provided by the incoming traffic. Additionally, one of the main functions of an XML gateway is to provide a robust defense against XML attacks that target the XML parser; XML gateways provide a robust system for detecting and validating XML traffic before it reaches the Web service and can be configured to notify appropriate personnel when such an attack has been attempted.

6.3 Languages for Secure Web Service Development

Each of the languages discussed in this section has its own set of sound security-related practices, but all benefit from a common set of secure coding practices that include the following:

- Do not include sensitive data in user-viewable source code (i.e., Web page code that can be displayed by the user using the *view source* function of his/her browser) or configuration files.
- Assemblies that support untrusted or partially trusted callers should never expose objects from assemblies that do not allow untrusted or partially trusted callers.
- Allow untrusted or partially trusted callers only after the developer has carefully reviewed the code, ascertained the security implications, and taken the necessary precautions to defend against attack.
- Disable tracing, debugging, and other diagnostic development or testing-related functions, tools, and hooks before application deployment.
- Do not issue verbose error information to the user.

6.3.1 Procedural Languages

The procedural languages summarized in the following sections are considered to be relevant to Web service design and development. This does not preclude the importance or relevance of other languages that are not explicitly described; rather, these are the languages most commonly used to implement Web services.

6.3.1.1 C and C++

There are many cases where Java, .NET, or other forms of managed code are not practical, even when implementing Web services. In particular, Web services based on C and C++ do not require the overhead of a framework to implement Web services specifications. Java EE and .NET can take up hundreds of megabytes of space, which may not be available on a particular system (usually a legacy or embedded system). When adding Web service support to legacy systems, Java and .NET may not be available, as .NET does not run on versions of Windows older than Windows 2000, and there may not be a Java Virtual Machine for the legacy system's platform or operating system.

To this end, there are a number of Web service frameworks available for C and C++. Web services developed using these frameworks do not have the security benefits provided by managed code such as .NET and Java, so they must rely on operating system-level security support such as restricting user permissions and running the Web service within restricted environments. It is important to ensure that all code is properly written to avoid the potential pitfalls of the language, such as buffer overflows. C and C++ Web services can be implemented without much of the complexity of a Java or .NET Web service and would not be susceptible to vulnerabilities associated with the framework itself. An additional step that can be taken to protect Web services developed in C or C++ would be to place the Web service behind an XML gateway, which would filter XML attacks and protect the C or C++ system from external entities.

6.3.1.2 Java

Java runs in a secure virtual environment through the Java Security Manager (JSM), which provides a sandbox in which Java applications can run. Java also provides more stringent memory protections than C or C++, relying on garbage collection and references memory management in place of the more manual approach used by C and C++. Java allows the user to have almost full control of the virtual environment in which the Java bytecode is run. Java code intended for use on the client runs in a different environment, under a different trust model, than code on the server. There are common requirements, whether the Java code runs on the client or server. Input from untrusted sources should always be checked and filtered. Java code that inherits methods from parents, interfaces, or parents' interfaces also inherits vulnerabilities in those methods. For this reason, it is critical that the developer use inheritance with caution.

Because the Java language is compiled into a platform-independent bytecode format, much of the information contained in the original Java source code remains in the compiled bytecode. This makes decompilation by attackers easier for Java than natively compiled languages like C and C++. Bytecode obfuscation is a technique designed to help protect Java bytecodes from decompilation. Preventing bytecode decompilation is a countermeasure both against disclosure and tampering (i.e., confidentiality and integrity concerns).

Java bytecode must be able to undergo bytecode verification, which gives it a measure of protection against malicious code, and it is not possible to distribute the bytecode in a more secure form. Application of digital signatures to the native Java code (code signing) is intended to increase the security of the distribution process by providing a means of verification by the execution environment that the received Java code came from a trusted source and has not been tampered with en route.

The technique most often proposed for reducing this vulnerability is code obfuscation. Code obfuscation transforms the Java program to make it more difficult to understand, yet functionally identical to the original. The program produces the same results, though it may execute more slowly or have other side effects because of the code added to it by the obfuscation technique. Thus, there are trade-offs that must be considered between the security provided by code obfuscation and the execution time and space penalties imposed on the transformed program.

There are a number of COTS and public domain programs and utilities for performing code obfuscation. Some of these apply optimizations to the Java compiler, such as array and loop reordering and procedure inlining. Code obfuscation can be classified according to the kind of information the obfuscation technique targets and how it affects that target.

6.3.1.3 Microsoft's .NET Languages: C# and VB.NET

C# was developed by Microsoft as part of its .NET initiative to provide developers with the power of languages like Java and C++ for rapid application development. Like Java, C# runs in a secure environment through code access security, which provides a sandbox in which to run Common Language Runtime (CLR) applications, such as C# and VB.NET. C# applications also benefit from a garbage collection system, preventing most memory leaks from affecting C# applications. C# provides a more type-safe environment than C++, but unlike Java, C# applications support accessing raw memory—although this requires certain code access security permissions to be enabled. .NET's code access security offers security features similar to Java's, such as code signing, stringent access control and sandboxing.

Visual Basic .NET was released alongside of C# as a successor to the legacy Visual Basic language. While the VB.NET syntax is similar to the original Visual Basic language, VB.NET provides a fully object-oriented language in place of the COM-based language of Visual Basic. While Visual Basic has some security concerns, VB.NET's support of garbage collection, object-oriented design, code access security, and the .NET framework make VB.NET similar to C# and Java. Through the .NET framework and the CLR, C# and VB.NET have access to the same security libraries and both C# and VB.NET applications are subject to code access security.

As in Java, code written in C# or VB.NET can be downloaded and run from untrusted sources. To alleviate this problem, Microsoft has integrated code access security into the .NET Framework. Code access security provides varying levels of trust for code based on where the code originates and allows individual users to specify what permissions will be given to an application. Because code access security is part of the .NET Framework, all applications that access the .NET Framework can be subject to code access security. Because policies are defined on a per-machine basis, libraries are provided that allow applications to determine whether the application has a particular permission prior to performing a potentially restricted act—allowing .NET applications to alter their behavior rather than simply generate a security exception.

6.3.2 XML

Content within SOAP messages is expressed in XML. Because of this, the security technologies used by Web services are based on those developed for XML. XML was designed so that it could be easily extensible and combined with itself. It should be natural to provide integrity, confidentiality and other security benefits to entire XML documents or portions of these documents in a way that does not prevent further processing by standard XML tools.

In general, most of the risks posed by XML are not unique. They can appear with many other technologies and systems, new and old. Some of the risks are more severe for XML than for older systems simply because XML is more expressive, flexible and powerful. Some of the risks derive from the ways in which XML is used (e.g., for metadata) and would appear whether using XML or some other technology.

Some recognized vulnerabilities and attacks specific to XML and XML Style Sheets (XSL) include the inability to:

- **Prove validity of XML content and originator.** Not all XML parsers validate the URIs of entity references before accessing them
- **Prevent exploitation of XML entities to steal information.** Because some parsers reference entities without first validating their URIs, it may be possible to inject references to other locations on the target server from which secret information could then be extracted
- **Prevent exploitation of XML entities to launch DoS attacks.** Because some parsers reference entities without first validating their URIs, it may be possible to create DoS attacks by flooding the XML parser with illegitimate entity references
- **Enforce validation.** An attacker may be able to subvert the validate command called by the XML application when it has loaded the schema cache with namespaces. Attackers do this by using a root element from a different namespace to redirect xsi:schemaLocation to point to their own schema, in which they include the declaration `<xs:any namespace=##any,, processContents="skip"/>`.

6.4 Security Testing: Tools and Techniques

Security testing in the Web services realm should be included in the overall test plan, and should be performed iteratively throughout the Web service's lifecycle, not just after implementation or deployment. The characteristics of Web services make security testing more difficult than for more traditional applications. The Web services model provides a completely implementation-independent mechanism through which applications can interact. The tester can make no accurate assumptions about how that application software is built. Thus, the reliance on black box testing is much heavier than it is for other application testing. Testers must also rely heavily for their understanding of the software on its interface and system specifications.

The highly distributed nature of Web services technology creates a dependence on complex interactions, which must be testable. The tester will need to adopt new techniques and processes for many aspects of Web services security testing. Security function testing in particular will require greater use of distributed test agents and associated technology, comparable to how load testing is done.

How much security-focused testing is enough? Ideally, the tester would trace all paths through the code and all internal interfaces among components within the service and all external interfaces between the service and other services, and would try out every possible input to ensure it didn't cause an unexpected security violation. Depending on the complexity of the service, testing every possible path, interface, and input may not be feasible. A more practical goal is to cover every path through each unit, and every inter-unit and external interface at least once.

Each of the categories of Web services security tests is discussed below.

- **Web Service Security Protocol Conformance Testing.** This type of testing is generally performed by an independent testing organization on specific implementations of Web services security protocols by specific vendors in their Web service products, as well as some open source implementations. The objective of this testing is to ensure that individual protocol implementations conform to the relevant published standards from OASIS or W3C.
- **Correctness Testing of Web Service Security Functionality.** This type of testing is focused on ensuring that the security functionality performed by a Web service meets its stated requirements.
- **Security Focused Unit Testing.** This type of testing focuses on the smallest unit of the Web service application, such as individual classes or functions, apart from the rest of the application. Through

unit testing, it is considerably easier to test all of the possible paths that attackers could take to reach unexposed methods or perform illegal operations.

- **Whole-Application Vulnerability Assessment.** The objective of this testing is to seek residual vulnerabilities that appear in the Web service as a whole, as a result of the interactions between the service and other Web services, instead of tracking down vulnerabilities within and among individual unit components of a single Web service.
- **Web Service Software Security Assessment**. This type of testing usually includes threat modeling, requirements risk analysis, and security modeling. Software security test techniques include security-oriented code reviews, security fault injection tests, fuzz testing, and penetration testing.

From a security standpoint, Web services adoption today is focused on the corporate intranet, with Web services used to simplify and reduce the cost of integration of existing applications and databases behind the firewall. Web services that communicate outside the firewall are showing up in pilot projects, but are typically limited to service interactions with trusted business partners and known IT organizations.

Given this current state of the art, three capabilities are important in the tools used for testing the security of Web services:

- Generation and testing of SOAP and XML messages, with examination of both messaging interfaces and individual message format
- Automatic generation of test plans from WSDL files containing metadata about the interfaces of the Web services to be tested
- Simulation of the actions of both requesters and providers.

There is little automated tool support specifically designed for Web services security testing. This dearth is consistent with the relatively small number of automated software and application security testing tools in general. This said, current Web services security testers will need to rely on the somewhat more prevalent software security testing and application vulnerability assessment techniques and tools to fill in the gaps until a more complete, robust set of Web service specific security testing tools emerges.

Tools for security testing of groups of Web services interacting across SOAs do not yet exist, nor do tools for testing security of Web services that are dynamically defined at runtime (e.g., through orchestration or choreography).

6.5 Summary

Web services provide interoperability among a variety of development platforms and operating systems, giving organizations flexibility when implementing them. To maximize this flexibility, it is important to understand the security benefits provided by some of the most widely used Web service development languages and what tools are available in those languages to aid in the development of Web services. Web service toolkits can prove to be essential to developing secure Web services, particularly if they are WS-I Basic Profile and WS-I Basic Security Profile compliant—allowing for interoperability with little or no change to the code generated by the toolkit. In addition, a robust XML parser is essential for developing Web services to prevent attacks designed to compromise the parser.

There are several languages commonly used to develop Web services: Java, C#, VB.NET, C, and C++. Java, C#, and VB.NET rely on managed code frameworks to provide many of the support functions necessary to implement Web services. C and C++ can provide performance improvements over their managed code counterparts and may be the only option when Web service-enabling a legacy application.

Regardless of what language is being used, the use of secure software development techniques is essential to preventing a number of vulnerabilities from being introduced into the Web service. To minimize the number of vulnerabilities in a Web service, testing tools and techniques can be used to perform penetration testing, functionality testing, source code review, and other tests. Through the use of WS-I compliant toolkits, secure software development practices, and security testing, it is possible to implement secure Web services that will withstand a wide variety of attacks.

Appendix A—Common Attacks Against Web Services

The following are common attacks targeting vulnerabilities often found in Web services. With exceptions noted in brackets, Web services are subject to these attacks.

A.1 Reconnaissance Attacks

Reconnaissance attacks have the objective of collecting information about an application and its execution environment to better target other types of attacks at that application. There are no standards for preventing reconnaissance attacks. UDDI v3.0.2 provides some protection against reconnaissance attacks by requiring identification, authentication and authorization of entities prior to granting access to the registry. Other discovery standards, such as WSDL, can be accessed by any entity and the information may be used in reconnaissance attacks. It is important to ensure that only authorized entities can gain access to discovery information, to Web service interfaces, and to Web service messages in transit.

A.1.1 Code Templates

The use of code templates and comments in code can provide information about the backend systems or the development environment of the Web application. Specifically, the use of template code can prove to be dangerous. This code can be obtained from many sources and can contain bugs that are easily identified in the source code. This information can be used to exploit a specific vulnerability or narrow the focus of vulnerability scans performed on the system.

A.1.2 Forceful Browsing Attack

Forceful browsing attacks attempt to detect Web services that are not explicitly publicized. An example of forceful browsing is an intruder making repeated requests to the Web service with the URL patterns of typical Web application components such as common gateway interface (CGI) programs. Depending on error messages received, this technique can be used to gain information about the unpublicized Web service.

A.1.3 Directory Traversal Attack

A directory traversal attack is closely related to a forceful browsing attack. Directory traversal occurs when an attacker tries to access restricted files used by a Web service. Usually, the requested files reside outside of the Web service host's normal file system directory, but they can also include resources within the service's host server that are restricted from being accessed by the attacker. Directory traversal attacks against Web services can be used to access the host server's password files or to access executables on the server to execute arbitrary commands.

A.1.4 WSDL Scanning

This type of attack is comparable to a directory traversal. Web Services Definition Language (WSDL) is an advertising mechanism for Web services to dynamically describe the parameters used when connecting with specific methods. These files are often built automatically using utilities. These utilities, however, are designed to expose and describe all of the information available in a method. A knowledgeable attacker may be able to locate Web services that have been removed from the pregenerated WSDL and subsequently access them.

A.1.5 Registry Disclosure Attacks

Attackers can use misconfigured registries (LDAP, X.500, etc.) to obtain information about the Web service being attacked. In particular, these registries can contain authentication information that an attacker may be able to use. Attackers can also use UDDI and ebXML registries to obtain information about the Web service being attacked. Important points of information disclosure are the WSDL descriptions in the UDDI or ebXML registry, and the registry's audit logs. Further, these registries can be compromised or corrupted, which may allow an attacker to gain information about the Web service's host or even gain access to that host.

A.2 Privilege Escalation Attacks

The objective of privilege escalation attempts is to enable the attacker to change the privilege level of a process, thereby taking control of that now-compromised process to bypass security controls that would otherwise limit the attacker's access to the Web service's functionality, data, resources, and environment. Web services are often configured to run with specific group or user permissions unrelated to those of the end user (human or requester service) responsible for causing the service's execution (e.g., "anonymous" or "nobody" permissions). Such Web services, if they also suffer from buffer overflows or race conditions, can be used to increase the permissions grabbed by the attacker, or to escalate the attacker's ability to cause damage to the Web service, its data, resources, or environment.

Attackers can perform privilege escalation by taking advantage of defects in the implementation, design, or configuration of Web services. Any standard developed to prevent privilege escalation attempts would remain susceptible to implementation, design, or configuration defects.

A.2.1 Dictionary Attack

Many systems have weak password protection and Web service interfaces are no different. Unlike Web portals, XML Web service interfaces are heterogeneous in nature with each system having its own authentication system and methods for deterring undesired behavior. Dictionary attacks are common where an attacker may either manually or programmatically attempt common passwords to gain entry into a system or multiple systems. Administrators should ensure that passwords are difficult to guess and are changed often. Unlike standard user credentials, application credentials are determined by the administrator. Password strengthening rules that are desirable for users should also apply to administrators of Web service interfaces.

A.2.2 Format String Attacks

Format string vulnerabilities are caused by programmer errors. For example, a C programmer may mean to type:

```
printf(buf, "%s", str);
```

but instead types:

```
printf(buf, str);
```

When the C code is compiled, it executes exactly as the programmer expected. Because the programmer left out the format string ("%s"), *printf* will interpret the string *str* to be the format string. This defect can be exploited by the attacker to compromise the program.

To exploit a format string vulnerability, the attacker sends unexpected inputs to the program in the form of strings specifically crafted to cause a privileged program to enable privilege escalation by a normal user. The format string vulnerability can then trick the privileged program into allowing arbitrary data to be written to the stack, thus enabling the attacker to take control of the program and the host on which it runs.

A.2.3 Buffer Overflow Exploits

Buffer overflow exploits are targeted at Web service components (most often those written in C or C++) that accept data as input and store it in memory (rather than on disk) for later use or manipulation. An overflow of a memory buffer results when the Web service component fails to adequately check the size of the input data to ensure that it is not larger than the memory buffer allocated to receive it, and instead passes the too-large data into the too-small buffer. The result is that the excess data is written into other areas of memory that are not prepared to receive it. Buffer overflows are particularly dangerous when those other areas of memory are allocated to store executable code rather than passive data—for example, an overflow of data onto the Web service program's execution stack.

If the oversized data input to the Web service component includes embedded spurious commands or malicious code, the buffer overflow may result in a loading of the malicious code into the service's execution stack. The stack will then execute the malicious code instead of the valid Web service code that was displaced from the stack by the buffer overflow. Spurious commands planted in this way are usually designed to grant privileges to the malicious code that exceed the service program's authorized permissions (possibly even granting administrator-level or root level permissions), thus granting the attack code—and through it, the attacker—access to data and control of resources and processes that would never have been granted to the displaced service code. Some buffer overflow attacks have a much simpler objective: they are designed to crash the service or suspend its execution (i.e., to achieve a DoS).

There are four basic approaches to defending against buffer overflow vulnerabilities and attacks:

- **Safe programming.** Write all Web service code in languages that automatically perform input validation, such as Java and C#, or if writing in C or C++, ensure that all expected input lengths and formats are explicitly specified, and that all inputs received are validated to ensure that they do not exceed those lengths or violate those formats. Error and exception handling should be expressly programmed to reject or truncate any inputs that violate the allowable input lengths/formats.
- **Memory allocation countermeasures.** By allocating only non-executable storage areas for input buffers, any attack code embedded in oversized inputs will not be inadvertently executed. This approach can be used to stop those buffer overflow attacks that have the objective of executing malicious code, but will not counteract buffer overflow DoS attacks.
- **Compiler-based countermeasures.** Several leading C and C++ compilers include antioverflow countermeasures that ensure that source code has array bounds checks performed at compile time on all array accesses. This method completely eliminates the buffer overflow problem by making overflows impossible, but imposes substantial overhead on the compilation process. Other compile-time countermeasures perform integrity checks on code pointers to buffers before dereferencing those pointers. This technique does not make buffer overflows impossible, but it does stop the majority of buffer overflow attacks and makes the attacks that it cannot stop difficult to achieve. These countermeasures have significant compatibility and performance advantages over compiler array bounds checking.
- **Library-based countermeasures.** Safe libraries that replace, at link time, commonly used but overflow-prone standard C and C++ functions are available, as are filtering/wrapping mechanisms for

adding safe logic (bounds definition and checking logic) to otherwise overflow-prone functions. Libsafe is the best known example of an antioverflow library-based countermeasure.

A.2.4 Race Conditions

Race conditions most often arise when multiple processes simultaneously attempt to access a shared resource (such as a file or variable), and these multiple access attempts have not been expected by the developer (i.e., the appropriate controls and checks to avoid such conflicts have not been implemented). Race conditions can be triggered intentionally by an attacker who uses the Web service in a way that causes it to spawn a large number of multiple processes that attempt to access the same file.

In object-oriented programming, it is important to verify within the program code that race conditions are minimized; this is done by not sharing common variables among object instances. Instead, the developer allocates a unique variable for each object instance. When global variables are used, they should be general values that cannot be changed by individual subroutines or functions; instead, the values are passed via references and stored in local variables. For each file access, the program is written to verify that the file is free before opening it. The program also includes logic for checking for and handling object-in-use errors. If the Web service accesses a database, it does so using appropriate transaction-oriented code.

A.2.5 Symlink Attacks

Symbolic links (symlinks) are links on Unix and Linux systems that point from one file to another file. A symlink vulnerability is exploited by making a symbolic link from a file to which an attacker does have access, to a file to which the attacker does not have access. The objective of the symlink attack is to trick a Web service program that has access rights to a given file into acting as a *de facto* proxy on the attacker's behalf by operating on (modifying or deleting) a file on which the program would not otherwise operate. Symlink attacks are often coupled with timing (race condition) attacks. Symlinks do not exist on Windows systems, so symlink attacks cannot be performed against programs/files on those systems.

A.2.6 Exploiting Unprotected Administrator Interfaces

Many Web services have administrative interfaces that contain vulnerabilities. Typical vulnerabilities in local and remote administration interfaces include:

- **Incorrectly configured access control security levels.** If the access controls on the administration interface are set too low (e.g., equal to user-level access), an attacker who manages to gain less-than-administrator privileges may be able to access and exploit the administration interface.
- **Incorrectly configured SSL security levels.** If the SSL is configured incorrectly, it may not achieve cryptographic separation of administrator sessions/tunnels from user sessions/tunnels. In addition, incorrectly configured SSL may not perform client or server authentication as expected, allowing for man-in-the-middle attacks.
- **Authentication of administrators.** When using HTTP Basic Authentication or HTML Form Authentication without SSL, the administrator's password is transmitted between the administrator's client and the Web service host in unencrypted form. If intercepted, the attacker gains access not just to administrator-accessible data, but also to privileged processes, configuration files, and security files. While the HTTP Digest Authentication does not send the administrator's password in cleartext form, the attacker can simply retransmit the digest to gain access to the service.

- **Internal, informative application error messages returned to users.** Such messages, if intercepted, can provide important reconnaissance information to attackers. To prevent this, all error messages should be logged and redirected via an SSL-encrypted connection to the administrator. In place of the original error message, an uninformative generic error message should be provided to all other users.

A.3 Attacks on Confidentiality

The objective of a confidentiality attack is to force the targeted application to disclose information that the attacker is not authorized to see, including sensitive information and private information. The XML Encryption, WS-Security, and HTTPS standards provide confidentiality protection for Web services. WS-Security and HTTPS are generally used to protect confidentiality of SOAP messages in transit, leaving data at rest vulnerable to attack. Because most Web service data is stored in the form of XML, using XML Encryption before storing data should provide confidentiality protection while maintaining compatibility. Other forms of data may be encrypted using AES, as defined in FIPS 197[57], or public key algorithms such as RSA, ElGamal, and ECC. Confidentiality attacks can also be aimed at subverting the Web service itself or the business process it is part of. To prevent such attacks, Web service designs and configurations should be reviewed by a third party and the developers should practice secure software development techniques.

A.3.1 Sniffing

Sniffing, or eavesdropping, is the act of monitoring network traffic exchanged between Web services to capture sensitive plaintext data such as unencrypted passwords and security configuration information transmitted in SOAP, UDDI, WSDL, and other such messages. With a simple packet sniffer, an attacker can easily read all plaintext traffic. Also, attackers can crack packets encrypted by lightweight algorithms and decipher the payload that the Web service developer considers to be secure. The sniffing of packets requires inserting a packet sniffer into the path between the service-to-service (or portal-to-service) traffic flow.

A.4 Attacks on Integrity

The objective of an integrity attack is to exploit the targeted application to make unauthorized changes to information accessed/handled by the application. Web service standards for protecting the integrity of data include WS-Security, XML Signature. Through cryptography, services can determine whether a particular SOAP message has been tampered with. Other tools and standards, such as FIPS 197, FIPS 186-2, and HTTPS, provide similar functionality for non-XML content. Due to Web services' reliance on XML, integrity attacks are not limited to altering messages in transit or data in storage. Integrity attacks can be aimed at the integrity of the Web service itself or the business process it is part of. To prevent such attacks, Web service designs and configurations should be reviewed by a third party and the developers should practice secure software development techniques.

A.4.1 Parameter Tampering

In a Web service, arbitrary data can be passed as parameters to Web service methods. These parameters may have been thought to be immutable within the Web service. If sufficient verification mechanisms are not in place, this leads to possible attacks. An example of a verification mechanism is the establishment of constraints on type and format in the WSDL file, then verifying that the correct type and format was received by the Web service.

---

[57] FIPS 197, *Advanced Encryption Standard*, is available at http://csrc.nist.gov/publications/fips/.

A.4.2 Schema Poisoning

XML schemas provide formatting instructions for parsers when interpreting XML documents. Schemas are used for all of the major XML standard grammars coming out of OASIS. Because these schemas describe necessary preprocessing instructions, they are susceptible to poisoning. An attacker may attempt to compromise the schema in its stored location and replace it with a similar but modified one that will either cause valid XML documents to be rejected, or cause invalid or malicious XML documents to be accepted by the application.

Similarly, such attacks can be used to manipulate data if the data types described in the schema are also compromised (e.g., by changing dates to integers when the Web service is performing arithmetic operations, or by modifying the data encoding to enable obfuscation of data that will eventually reach the XML parser and be reformed into attack code, similar to the way a Unicode attack traverses directories via Web servers).

A.4.3 Spoofing of UDDI/ebXML Messages

Dense groups of UDDI or ebXML *garbage* data can obscure query results related to specific providers. Garbage data within UDDI is defined as useless data either intentionally or carelessly added by users via the publish API defined in the Programmers API Specification. This garbage, if permitted to collect at too great a rate, can shut down one or more UDDI operators. For example, a vast amount of data could be added to UDDI as a form of a denial of service attack upon the registry. Similarly, UDDI entries may be added that reference malicious Web services; without proper protections in place, requesters may access such malicious Web services assuming they can be trusted.

Another possible target of attack is the UDDI or ebXML registry used for discovery of Web services. This registry is a directory (comparable to an LDAP or X.500 directory) or database, which is vulnerable to the same types of attacks as other directories and databases, particularly in terms of integrity and availability. It is possible to conceive of a cross-site scripting attack in which a Web service's entry in a UDDI or ebXML registry is compromised to direct the unsuspecting user to a bogus Web service (i.e., spoofing).

A.4.4 Checksum Spoofing

The attacker intercepts and updates a message with a hash attached as an integrity mechanism, recomputes the hash (guessing the algorithm that was used to compute the original hash) and applies it to the altered message, then forwards that message to the intended destination. The provider processes the message, running the plaintext of the message ("Place 100 orders") through the hashing algorithm to recompute the hash, which will be equal to whatever the attacker computed.

A.4.5 Principal Spoofing

In this attack, a false message is sent which appears to be from a requester. For example, the attacker sends a message that appears as though it is from a valid requester service. Countermeasures for spoofing require correctly configuring perimeter security, such as rejecting incoming packets from the Internet that contain an internal (behind the firewall) IP address in their header, as well as rejecting outgoing packets when their headers indicate that the packets originated from an external IP address (outside the firewall).

A.4.6 Routing Detours

The WS-Addressing specification provides a way to direct XML traffic through a complex environment. It operates by allowing an interim way station in an XML path to assign routing instructions to an XML document. If one of these Web services way stations is compromised, it may participate in a man-in-the-middle attack by inserting bogus routing instructions to point a confidential document to a malicious location. From that location, it may be possible to forward on the document to its original destination after stripping out the malicious instructions.

A.4.7 External Entity Attack

XML enables a requester to construct an XML document into which data is dynamically inserted at the time of document creation by pointing to the URI of the data store where the needed data resides. If that data store is not established to be trustworthy (i.e., if the requester service fails to authenticate the data store or validate the source of the data), an attacker may be able to reroute the requests for data to an entity he controls to return malicious content instead of valid data. Additionally, the attacker could intercept the XML data returned by the valid but untrusted data store and replace or augment that data with malicious content, which will then be included by the requester in the dynamically constructed XML document.

A.4.8 Canonicalization

Different forms of input that resolve to the same standard name (the canonical name) is referred to as canonicalization. Web service code is particularly susceptible to a canonicalization attack if it makes security decisions based on the name of a resource that is passed to it as input. Files, pathnames, URLs/URIs, and user names are the most frequently targeted resources vulnerable to canonicalization; in each case there are many different ways to represent the same name. The Web service should require all input names to be converted to their canonical forms prior to being used by the service to make security decisions, such as whether access should be granted or denied to the specified file indicated by the canonical name.

A.4.9 Intelligent Tampering and Impersonation

This category of attack refers to attacks in which the attacker attempts to spoof a trusted server or service by impersonating or tampering with a legitimate program.

Intelligent tampering refers to topologies in which the intruder modifies the Web service program or its data in some specific way that allows the service to continue to operate in a way that seems normal, but which actually reflects a subverted state or uses corrupted data. For example, overwriting the service program's data buffers with data that is in the correct format but has different-than-expected values is an example of intelligent tampering. Tampering with the Web service software in a random way (e.g., overwriting random bits in the memory) does not constitute an intelligent tampering attack, although it may result in a denial of service as the tampered program or data can cause execution to fail.

An impersonation attack is similar to intelligent tampering in that the attacker seeks to establish a rogue version of the legitimate Web service program. Whereas intelligent tampering usually involves direct modifications to the internal specifics (e.g., code, data) of the program, impersonation attempts to emulate the observable behavior of the program while subverting its internal state.

A.5 Denial of Service Attacks

A direct attack on availability, a DoS attack prevents the service provider from receiving or responding to messages from a requester. Because Web service interfaces are heterogeneous, it takes knowledge about the underlying Web service applications to protect them against DoS attacks. For example, a Web service that provides simple query responses might be able to handle 1,000 requests per second, while a financial system made up of a series or collection of services that collaboratively perform complex financial transactions might only be able to handle five requests per hour because of the complexity of the series of calculations involved. While sending ten requests per hour to the query application would not degrade its performance at all, intentionally sending ten requests per hour to a financial system that is known or suspected to be incapable of handling such a load would constitute a DoS attack.

DoS attacks such as these would not be detected by a firewall or an intrusion detection system (IDS), mainly because these countermeasures do not provide the granularity necessary to control DoS on a per-transaction/operation basis, and also because these countermeasures tend to be either entry-point or per-host specific. Without sophisticated collection, correlation, and analysis tools, they will not be able to detect DoS attacks specifically launched against a series of services. Only an understanding of real-world usage can prepare the administrator to compile profile information on each Web service so that countermeasures can be correctly selected and configured to protect each service from DoS attacks.

Two competing standards to support reliable Web service messaging are available. The OASIS WS-Reliability standard was released in November 2004, while the BEA, IBM, Microsoft, and TIBCO WS-ReliableMessaging standard was released in February 2005. Both standards provide a mechanism to guarantee that messages are sent and received in a SOA. What is lacking are standards that define how Web services should react to DoS and how QoS should be handled within a SOA. There are standards for QoS and techniques for handling DoS in lower layer protocols like IP, but SOAP messages can be transmitted in multiple IP packets, requiring standards and techniques specifically for Web services. Increasingly, XML gateways are being used to augment widely accepted techniques because they are capable of detecting and preventing XML-based DoS.

A.5.1 Flooding Attacks

Flooding attacks most often involve copying valid service requests and resending them to a provider. The attacker may issue repetitive SOAP/XML messages in an attempt to overload the Web service. This type of activity may not be detected as an intrusion because the source IP address will be valid, the network packet behavior will be valid, and the SOAP/XML message will be well-formed. The business behavior will not be legitimate and constitutes a DoS attack.

Techniques for detecting and handling DoS can be applied against flooding attacks. In some ways, flooding attacks against Web services are easier to detect than those against Web applications, because Web service payload information is more readily available. With the right tools, message traffic patterns indicating possible DoS attacks can be detected even when the same or similar payload is being sent via multiple communications protocols (e.g., HTTP, HTTPS, SMTP, or across different physical or logical interfaces).

A.5.2 Recursive Payloads Sent to XML Parsers

One of the strengths of XML is its ability to nest elements within a document to address the need for complex relationships among elements. XML is valuable for forms that have a form name or purpose that contains many different value elements, such as a purchase order that incorporates shipping and billing addresses as well as various items and quantities ordered. We can intuitively acknowledge the value of nesting elements three or four levels, perhaps more. An attacker can easily create a document that attempts to stress and break an XML parser by creating a document that is 10,000 or 100,000 elements deep.

A.5.3 Oversized Payloads Sent to XML Parsers

XML is verbose by design in its markup of existing data and information, so file size must always be considered. While an enterprise's programmers and analysts will work to limit the size of a document, there are a number of reasons to have XML documents that are hundreds of megabytes or gigabytes in size. Sometimes this is a function of converting a batch file transfer process into a realtime process. It may also occur in the multimedia (e.g., digital video) world where gigabyte files are the norm. Or, it could be an attacker again exercising the parser to execute a DoS attack. Parsers based on the document object model, which represent the entire XML document in memory, are especially susceptible to this attack, given their need to model the entire document in memory prior to parsing. Coercive parsing, discussed above, is an example of sending an oversized payload.

A.5.4 Schema Poisoning

In addition to attacking confidentiality (see Appendix A.4.2), schema poisoning can be used to perform a DoS attack. Attacks against the grammar of an XML file can be easily achieved if the XML schema is compromised.

XML documents need to conform to the protocols and specifications governing their use. It is common for attackers to attempt to manipulate documents contrary to those rules to conduct a DoS attack or compromise external sources. For example, a perfectly formed XML document may be inappropriate and undesirable to a specific Web service if it contains policy violations such as excessive size, inclusion of inappropriate or unexpected values, or data dependencies within the content. WSDL files and schemas may be enumerated or spoofed with similar objectives.

A.5.5 Memory Leak Exploitation

Memory leaks occur when a program dynamically allocates memory space for an object, array, or variable of some other type, but fails to free up the space before the program finishes executing. Repeated over time, memory leaks can cause the program to allocate all available memory (physical memory and paging file space), with the result that all software processes on the allocating program's host suspend operation until the allocating program releases the memory. Memory leaks can be exploited by attackers by inserting malicious code that is written to hog memory resources and cause DoS.

Memory leaks are most common in programs that allocate arrays and variable data types. It is important to write programs that always deallocate local arrays before terminating execution of subroutines. Global arrays should be deallocated whenever they are not being used. Some widgets, such as Data Access Object (DAO) components and computing grid components, may include memory leaks if their properties are not handled correctly. Memory leaks provide an easy entry point for buffer overflow attacks.

A.6 Command Injection

In a command injection, executable logic is inserted in non-executable text strings submitted to a provider/provider Web service. The main types of command injection are SQL injection targeting Web service-enabled database applications, and XML injection targeting Web services. Common command injection attacks are described below. Command injections are usually the result of a design, implementation, or configuration defect. Most commonly, command injections result in Web services that do not validate input before processing it. Any standard designed to prevent command injections would be susceptible to the same defects. XML gateways provide some protection against command injection by scanning SOAP messages prior to passing them on to their intended destination. To prevent command injections, Web service designs and configurations should be reviewed by a third party and the developers should practice secure software development techniques.

A.6.1 SQL Injection

SQL injection is a technique used for manipulating Web services that send SQL queries to a RDBMS to alter, insert, or delete data in a database. RDBMSs communicate with Web services via service interface application logic that creates a communication channel between the frontend Web service and the backend RDBMS.

The main vulnerability that enables Web service-enabled RDBMSs to be attacked in this way is the common practice of configuring the backend RDBMS to accept and execute any valid SQL query received from any user (including a Web service frontend) that has the necessary access privileges. Should an attacker hijack a valid authenticated interface from the frontend Web service to the backend RDBMS, the attacker would be able to perform any valid SQL query. Such an attack does require the attacker to have fairly deep knowledge of how the Web service-enabled database application has been implemented.

SQL injection attacks are most effectively prevented by applying thorough application-layer countermeasures, such as Web application firewalls, and better yet, by explicitly designing and implementing the Web service logic added to legacy database applications to resist/reject all input that contains SQL injection attack patterns. Network-level firewalls and IDS, and database security controls have not proved effective in defending against SQL injection attacks.

The main modes of SQL injection are:

- **Data manipulation.** The attacker intercepts and manipulates the data sent from a Web service to the RDBMS, most often to bypass the RDBMS's authentication process. For example, the attacker may modify an intercepted SQL statement by adding elements to the *WHERE* clause of the Web service's authentication statement so the *WHERE* clause always results in *TRUE*, or by extending the SQL statement to include set operators like *UNION, INTERSECT,* or *MINUS*. Another method involves manipulating or executing *UPDATE, INSERT, DELETE,* or *DROP* statements to alter information to exceed the privileges granted to the originating service.
- **Command execution.** The attacker uses the RDBMS to execute SQL-specific system-level commands.

In a SQL injection attack, the attacker inserts new SQL statements or database commands into an intercepted SQL statement, for example, to append a Transact-SQL *EXECUTE* command to the intercepted SQL statement. SQL injections are most often successful when targeting databases that allow multiple SQL statements to be appended to a single database request. Most RDBMSs are vulnerable to this type of multi-statement attack, and the Transact-SQL *EXECUTE* statement is the most frequent target of SQL injections. While other databases may not support the *EXECUTE* statement, all database applications can dynamically execute SQL queries, and such queries, depending on how the application constructs them, may be vulnerable to attack.

SQL injection attacks do not require the attacker to have deep knowledge of the targeted application, and thus can be easily automated. The attacker inserts customized statements into the intercepted SQL query to make operating system calls or to manipulate data in the database. Some attacks may target vulnerabilities associated with the RDBMS itself, such as a buffer overflow. Patches for all known RDBMS vulnerabilities should be downloaded and applied to production databases regularly.

INSERT, *UPDATE*, or *DELETE* statements can be used to modify data in the database. An attacker may also route information from the database to a remote computer. Many SQL applications leverage packages of stored procedures, which may be exploited by an attacker if they provide functionality to change passwords or perform other sensitive transactions.

Dynamically generated SQL statements, which are commonly used in Web service-enabled database applications, are particularly vulnerable to SQL injection attacks. For example, a dynamic SQL statement used to request a page on a SOA portal could be manipulated to insert other SQL statements in the URL/URI pointing to that portal page, such as statements to retrieve information from the database and sends it to the portal via the database application's Web service frontend that interfaces with the portal. Because most database servers are deployed behind a firewall, this form of SQL injection can also be used to attack other hosts and applications on the internal network. As noted earlier, custom stored procedures can also be executed in this way.

A.6.2 XML Injection

XML injection can occur when user input is passed directly into an XML document or stream, similar to cross-site scripting or SQL injection. XML injection is often used to manipulate XPath queries to gain access to information in XML content that would otherwise be inaccessible to the attacker. XML injection may also target XQuery queries and XACML messages. Because XQuery is a successor to SQL, XML injections against XQuery can achieve objectives similar to those of SQL injection attacks. XML injections targeting XACML may allow the attacker to gain unauthorized access to other portions of the Web service (or its host) or modify the Web service's security policies. XML injection may also allow the attacker to perform the equivalent of a cross-site scripting attack, in which requesters of a valid Web service have their requests transparently rerouted to an attacker-controlled Web service.

A.6.3 Cross-Site Scripting

As noted in a previous section, an attacker may use XML injection to perform the equivalent of a cross-site scripting attack, in which requesters of a valid Web service have their requests transparently rerouted to an attacker-controlled Web service, most often one that performs malicious operations. UDDI references may be compromised through cross-site scripting, resulting in a reference to a malicious program instead of a valid Web service. Potential damages resulting from cross-site scripting attacks include:

- Exposure of SSL-encrypted connections
- Access to restricted Web services or resources via the attacked service
- Violation of domain security policies
- Rendering Web portal content returned by the attacked service unreadable or difficult to use, defacement of portal pages, addition to portal pages of annoying banners, popup windows, animations, offensive material
- Inserting spyware, malicious code, etc. into visiting browsers
- Violations of user privacy
- Causing DoS attacks (e.g., by continuously spawning new processes on the Web service host)

- Targeting specific vulnerabilities in scripting languages
- Causing buffer overflows.

A.7 Malicious Code Attacks

NOTE: This discussion focuses mainly on malicious code attacks against Web services in deployment. Countermeasures against insertion of malicious code into the Web service in development fall within the realm of configuration management practices, and are beyond the scope of this SP.

The objective of malicious code is to replace or augment the service's valid logic with malicious code that intentionally subverts or prevents the service's intended operation.

Malicious code attacks are most often achieved by including executable commands in what is expected to be non-executable input. In some cases, these commands provide pointers (links) to locations at which malicious code resides and from which, as soon as the location is accessed, it will be automatically downloaded to the targeted system. The following sections describe specific malicious code "delivery mechanisms" (attacks).

Tools and technologies to detect when an application has been subverted by malicious code or to prevent malicious code from entering a system are being researched. Such technologies would expand the definition of trust in Web services to include whether a particular entity is malicious. Until that point, malicious code attacks can be prevented by minimizing any other available attack vectors and by thoroughly validating input prior to processing it.

A.7.1 Command Injection

Attackers may take advantage of the command injection techniques discussed in Appendix A.6 to insert malicious code into a Web service. Command injection can result in running executable content on the Web service or inserting specially crafted data into the Web service's data store. Successfully injecting executable content may allow the attacker to gain full or partial control over the operation of the Web service, allowing for modification of any processing logic. Injecting specially crafted data may produce similar results. For example, an XML injection attack may cause the SOAP response from the now-malicious Web service to include extra XML content that will be interpreted by the requester to perform a specific action.

A.7.2 Malformed Content

This type of attack attempts to exploit the targeted Web service by discovering backdoors in its host platform. Many attackers attempt to elevate their privilege levels to incur further damage or gain further data from the service. Such attacks include inserting incorrectly formatted or otherwise invalid content into SOAP messages or their XML payloads destined for a Web service that does not perform input validation or adequate exception handling. Tampering with XML data and SOAP messages in transit can produce malformed content that is transmitted between services.

A.7.3 Logic Bombs, Trapdoors, and Backdoors

A logic bomb is malicious code that is left dormant until the Web service reaches a certain state, at which point the malicious code is executed. A trapdoor or backdoor is malicious code that has the specific objective of enabling the attacker (or the Web service that acts as a proxy service on the attacker's behalf) to bypass the targeted Web service's (or its host's) authentication mechanisms to gain access to sensitive data or resources, without being detected. Logic bombs, trapdoors, and backdoors are usually delivered as Trojan horses via another attack vector such as a virus or worm payload or planted by an attacker who has gained the necessary level of write-access to the Web service host.

Note that many logic bombs, backdoors, and trapdoors are planted by the developer of the Web service that contains them. Unlike external attackers, developers can exploit their deep knowledge of how a particular Web service's host will be configured in deployment, and how its system-, middleware-, and application-level components will interact.

Appendix B—ebXML

Electronic Business using eXtensible Markup Language (ebXML) was developed in 1999 by United Nations Centre for Trade Facilitation and Electronic Business (UN/CEFACT) and OASIS. Like Web services, ebXML was designed to use existing standards to enable cross-platform and interoperable business-to-business transactions. The goal of ebXML is to succeed the Electronic Data Interchange (EDI), which is a proprietary standard used for many of the business-to-business transactions performed today. ebXML provides an XML vocabulary for describing business processes, storing business processes in a registry, discovering business processes, developing a collaboration protocol agreement, and sending messages.

ebXML defines XML schema for defining business process and information models that can be stored in an ebXML registry. Businesses can then search an ebXML registry and for another business' details and develop, configure, or purchase software to interface with that business' ebXML interfaces and develop a Collaboration Protocol Agreement. Once initialized, all ebXML transactions occur via the ebXML Messaging Service.

The ebXML registry is comparable to a UDDI registry. Both allow businesses to discover one another to dynamically initiate business-to-business transactions. The ebXML registry provides a more structured environment, as it stores rigidly-defined business processes and related meta-data along with Collaboration Protocol Profiles. The similarities between ebXML and UDDI are apparent when looking at the design of the Java API for XML Registries (JAX-R), which abstracts UDDI and ebXML and provides a single API for both types of XML registries.

The ebXML Messaging Service is an extension of SOAP, meaning that ebXML provides a highly structured SOA. The ebXML Messaging Service extends SOAP to provide support for security, improved error handling, and reliable messaging. With these extensions, the ebXML Messaging Service can rely on a well-known and well-established protocol to perform sensitive and timely business transactions.

The ebXML specifications also take into account security. Both the ebXML Registry Services Specification and the ebXML Messaging Services Specification provide tools for ensuring the confidentiality and integrity of data within the system. The ebXML Registry supports storing digitally signed XML messages and uses authentication and authorization mechanisms to ensure that only appropriate entities access or update the registry. ebXML messaging supports encrypting and digitally signing SOAP messages and also provides a reliable messaging service to ensure the availability of messages.

Appendix C—Glossary

Selected terms used in the *Guide to Secure Web Services* are defined below. The sources of the definitions are listed at the end of the appendix.

Agent: A program acting on behalf of a person or organization. [1]

Attribute: A distinct characteristic of an object often specified in terms of their physical traits, such as size, shape, weight, and color, etc., for real-world objects. Objects in cyberspace might have attributes describing size, type of encoding, network address, etc. [1]

Attribute Based Access Control: An access control approach in which access is mediated based on attributes associated with subjects (requesters) and the objects to be accessed. Each object and subject has a set of associated attributes, such as location, time of creation, access rights, etc. Access to an object is authorized or denied depending upon whether the required (e.g., policy-defined) correlation can be made between the attributes of that object and of the requesting subject. [2]

Brokered Trust: Describes the case where two entities do not have direct business agreements with each other, but do have agreements with one or more intermediaries so as to enable a business trust path to be constructed between the entities. The intermediary brokers operate as active entities, and are invoked dynamically via protocol facilities when new paths are to be established. [3]

Choreography: Defines the requirements and sequences through which multiple Web services interact. [1]

Component: A software object, meant to interact with other components, encapsulating certain functionality or a set of functionalities. A component has a clearly defined interface and conforms to a prescribed behavior common to all components within an architecture. [1]

Conversation: Where Web services maintain some state during an interaction that involves multiple messages or participants. [1]

Coordination: Refers to the building, from a set of Web services, of something at a higher level, typically itself exposed as a larger Web service. Also referred to as "Composability." *Choreography* and *orchestration* are two approaches to coordination. [4]

Defense Discovery Metadata Standard (DDMS): Defines discovery metadata elements for resources posted to community and organizational shared spaces throughout the DoD enterprise. Specifically DDMS defines a set of information fields that are to be used to describe any data or service asset that is made known to the enterprise. [5]

Discovery: The act of locating a machine-processable description of a Web service-related resource that may have been previously unknown and that meets certain functional criteria. It involves matching a set of functional and other criteria with a set of resource descriptions. The goal is to find an appropriate Web service-related resource. [1]

Discovery Service: A service that enables agents to retrieve Web services-related resource description. [1]

Document Type Definition (DTD): A document defining the format of the contents present between the tags in an XML or SGML document, and the way they should be interpreted by the application reading the XML or SGML document. [6]

Electronic Business XML (ebXML): Sponsored by UN/CEFACT and OASIS, a modular suite of specifications that enable enterprises of any size and in any geographical location to perform business-to-business transactions using XML. [7]

Extensible Markup Language (XML): A cross-platform, extensible, and text-based standard markup language for representing structured data. It provides a cross-platform, software- and hardware-independent tool for transmitting information. [35]

Federated Trust: Trust established within a federation, enabling each of the mutually trusting realms to share and use trust information (e.g., credentials) obtained from any of the other mutually trusting realms. [10]

Federation: A collection of realms (domains) that have established trust among themselves. The level of trust may vary, but typically includes authentication and may include authorization. [10]

Framework: A layered structure indicating what kind of programs can or should be built and how they would interrelate. Some computer system frameworks also include actual programs, specify programming interfaces, or offer programming tools for using the frameworks. A framework may be for a set of functions within a system and how they interrelate; the layers of an operating system; the layers of an application subsystem; how communication should be standardized at some level of a network; and so forth. A framework is generally more comprehensive than a protocol and more prescriptive than a structure. [11]

Fuzz Testing: Similar to fault injection in that invalid data is input into the application via the environment, or input by one process into another process. Fuzz testing is implemented by tools called fuzzers, which are programs or script that submit some combination of inputs to the test target to reveal how it responds. [12]

HyperText Transfer Protocol over SSL/TLS (HTTPS): HTTP transmitted over TLS. [13]

Interface: In a service-oriented architecture, a specification of the operations that a service offers its clients. In WSDL 2.0 an interface component describes sequences of messages that a service sends or receives. In WSDL 1.1 an interface is specified in a portType element. [14]

Intermediary Service: A component that lies between the Service Client (subscriber) and the Service Provider (publisher). It intercepts the request from the Service Client, provides the service (functionality), and forwards the request to the Service Provider. Similarly, it intercepts the response from the Service Provider and forwards it to the Service Client. [15]

Kerberos: A means of verifying the identities of principals on an open network. Kerberos accomplishes this without relying on the authentication, trustworthiness, or physical security of hosts while assuming all packets can be read, modified and inserted at will. Kerberos uses a trust broker model and symmetric cryptography to provide authentication and authorization of users and systems on the network. [16]

Message: The basic unit of data sent from one Web services agent to another in the context of Web services. [1]

Obligation: An operation specified in a policy or policy set that should be performed by the PEP in conjunction with the enforcement of an authorization decision. [17]

Orchestration: Defines the sequence and conditions in which one Web service invokes other Web services to realize some useful function. An orchestration is the pattern of interactions that a Web service agent must follow to achieve its goal. [1]

Pairwise Trust: Establishment of trust by two entities that have direct business agreements with each other. [3]

Penetration Testing: A method of testing where testers target individual binary components or the application as a whole to determine whether intra or intercomponent vulnerabilities can be exploited to compromise the application, its data, or its environment resources. [12]

Policy: Statements, rules or assertions that specify the correct or expected behavior of an entity. For example, an authorization policy might specify the correct access control rules for a software component. [14]

Policy Based Access Control (PBAC): A strategy for managing user access to one or more systems, where the business roles of users is combined with policies to determine what access privileges users of each role should have. Theoretical privileges are compared to actual privileges, and differences are automatically applied. For example, a role may be defined for a manager. Specific types of accounts on the single sign-on server, Web server, and database management system may be attached to this role. Appropriate users are then attached to this role. [20]

Policy Decision Point (PDP): Mechanism that examines requests to access resources, and compares them to the policy that applies to all requests for accessing that resource to determine whether specific access should be granted to the particular requester who issued the request under consideration. [21]

Policy Enforcement Point (PEP): Mechanism (e.g., access control mechanism of a file system or Web server) that actually protects (in terms of controlling access to) the resources exposed by Web services. [21]

Provider: The entity (person or organization) that provides an appropriate agent, referred to as the "provider agent" to implement a particular Web service. It will use the provider agent to exchange messages with the requester's requester agent. "Provider" is also used as a shorthand to refer to the provider agent acting on the provider's behalf. [22]

Proxy: An agent that acts on behalf of a requester to relay a message between a requester agent and a provider agent. The proxy appears to the provider agent Web service to be the requester. [1]

Public Key Infrastructure (PKI): A set of policies, processes, server platforms, software and workstations used for the purpose of administering certificates and public-private key pairs, including the ability to issue, maintain, and revoke public key certificates. The PKI includes the hierarchy of certificate authorities that allow for the deployment of digital certificates that support encryption, digital signature and authentication to meet business and security requirements. [18], [7], [19]

Registry: An authoritative, centrally-controlled store of information. Web services use registries to advertise their existence and to describe their interfaces and other attributes. Prospective clients query registries to locate required services and to discover their attributes. [14]

Requester: The entity (person or organization) that wishes to make use of a provider's Web service. It will use a requester agent to exchange messages with the provider's provider agent. "Requester" is also used as a shorthand to refer to the requester agent acting on the requester's behalf. [22]

Risk-Adaptive Access Control (RAdAC): In RAdAC, access privileges are granted based on a combination of a user's identity, mission need, and the level of security risk that exists between the system being accessed and a user. RAdAC will use security metrics, such as the strength of the authentication method, the level of assurance of the session connection between the system and a user, and the physical location of a user, to make its risk determination. [23]

Role Based Access Control (RBAC): A model for controlling access to resources where permitted actions on resources are identified with roles rather than with individual subject identities. [24]

Sandbox: A system that allows an untrusted application to run in a highly controlled environment where the application's permissions are restricted to an essential set of computer permissions. In particular, an application in a sandbox is usually restricted from accessing the file system or the network. A widely used example of applications running inside a sandbox is a Java applet. [26]

Secure Sockets Layer (SSL): Provides privacy and reliability between two communicating applications. It is designed to encapsulate other protocols, such as HTTP. SSL v3.0 was released in 1996. It has been succeeded by IETF's TLS. [27]

Security Assertions Markup Language (SAML): A framework for exchanging authentication and authorization information. Security typically involves checking the credentials presented by a party for authentication and authorization. SAML standardizes the representation of these credentials in an XML format called *assertions*, enhancing the interoperability between disparate applications. [25]

Security Fault Injection Test: Involves data perturbation (i.e., alteration of the type of data the execution environment components pass to the application, or that the application's components pass to one another). Fault injection can reveal the effects of security defects on the behavior of the components themselves and on the application as a whole. [12]

Security-Oriented Code Review: A code review, or audit, investigates the coding practices used in the application. The main objective of such reviews is to discover security defects and potentially identify solutions. [12]

Security Service: A processing or communication service that is provided by a system to give a specific kind of protection to resources, where said resources may reside with said system or reside with other systems, for example, an authentication service or a PKI-based document attribution and authentication service. A security service is a superset of AAA services. Security services typically implement portions of security policies and are implemented via security mechanisms. [1]

Service: A software component participating in a service-oriented architecture that provides functionality or participates in realizing one or more capabilities. [14]

Service Composition: Aggregation of multiple small services into larger services. [14]

Service Description: A set of documents that describe the interface to and semantics of a service. [1]

Service Interface: The abstract boundary that a service exposes. It defines the types of messages and the message exchange patterns that are involved in interacting with the service, together with any conditions implied by those messages. [1]

Service-Oriented Architecture (SOA): A collection of services. These services communicate with each other. The communication can involve either simple data passing or it could involve two or more services coordinating some activity. [14]

SOAP: An XML-based protocol for exchanging structured information in a decentralized, distributed environment. [14]

SOAP Header: A collection of zero or more blocks of information prepended to a SOAP message, each of which might be targeted at any SOAP receiver within the message path. [1]

SOAP Message: The basic unit of communication between SOAP nodes. [1]

Transport Layer Security (TLS): Provides privacy and data integrity between two communicating applications. It is designed to encapsulate other protocols, such as HTTP. TLS v1.0 was released in 1999, providing slight modifications to SSL 3.0. [28]

Trust: The willingness to take actions expecting beneficial outcomes, based on assertions by other parties. [14]

Trust Relationships: Policies that govern how entities in differing domains honor each other's authorizations. An authority may be completely trusted—for example, any statement from the authority will be accepted as a basis for action—or there may be limited trust, in which case only statements in a specific range are accepted. [14]

Universal Description, Discovery, and Integration (UDDI): An XML-based lookup service for locating Web services in an Internet Topology. UDDI provides a platform-independent way of describing and discovering Web services and Web service providers. The UDDI data structures provide a framework for the description of basic service information, and an extensible mechanism to specify detailed service access information using any standard description language. [6]

Web Portal: Provides a single point of entry into the SOA for requester entities, enabling them to access Web services transparently from any device at virtually any location. [29]

Web Service: A software component or system designed to support interoperable machine- or application-oriented interaction over a network. A Web service has an interface described in a machine-processable format (specifically WSDL). Other systems interact with the Web service in a manner prescribed by its description using SOAP messages, typically conveyed using HTTP with an XML serialization in conjunction with other Web-related standards. [14]

Web Service Interoperability (WS-I) Basic Profile: A set of standards and clarifications to standards that vendors must follow for basic interoperability with SOAP products. [30]

Web Services Description Language (WSDL): An XML format for describing network services as a set of endpoints operating on messages containing either document-oriented or procedure-oriented information. WSDL complements the UDDI standard by providing a uniform way of describing the abstract interface and protocol bindings and deployment details of arbitrary network services. [32], [8]

Web Services Security (WS-Security): A mechanism for incorporating security information into SOAP messages. WS-Security uses binary tokens for authentication, digital signatures for integrity, and content-level encryption for confidentiality. [31]

XML Encryption: A process/mechanism for encrypting and decrypting XML documents or parts of documents. [33]

XML Information Security Marking (XML-ISM): Provides definitions of and implementation of the XML attributes used as containers for Controlled Access Program Coordination Office (CAPCO)-defined sensitivity and classification markings to be applied to all or part of an XML document. The markings are implemented using ICML. [34]

XML Schema: A language for describing the defining the structure, content and semantics of XML documents. [35]

XML Signature: A mechanism for ensuring the origin and integrity of XML documents. XML Signatures provide integrity, message authentication, or signer authentication services for data of any type, whether located within the XML that includes the signature or elsewhere. [35]

XPath: Used to define the parts of an XML document, using path expressions. [6]

XQuery: Provides functionality to query an XML document. [6]

The definitions above were derived from the following sources:

1. *Web Services Glossary - W3C Working Group Note 11 February 2004*, http://www.w3.org/TR/2004/NOTE-ws-gloss-20040211

2. *Common Criteria for Information Technology Security Evaluation (CC) Version 2.3, Part 2: Security Functional Components FDP_ACF.1*, http://www.commoncriteriaportal.org/public/files/ccpart2v2.3.pdf)

3. *OASIS Trust Models Guidelines*, http://www.oasis-open.org/committees/download.php/6158/sstc-saml-trustmodels-2.0-draft-01.pdf

4. Berners-Lee, Tim, *Web Services Program Integration across Application and Organization Boundaries (24 July 2004)*, http://www.w3.org/DesignIssues/WebServices.html

5. Defense Discovery Metadata Specification (DDMS) page, http://www.afei.org/news/ddms.pdf

6. Ananthamurthy, Lakshmi, *Web Services Glossary (developer.com 21 October 2002)*, http://www.developer.com/services/article.php/1485771

7. *OASIS Glossary of Terms*, http://www.oasis-open.org/glossary/index.php

8. *Oregon Statewide Automated Child Welfare Information System (SACWIS) Glossary*, http://egov.oregon.gov/DHS/children/data/sacwis/acronyms.shtml

9. *State of Maine Electronic Commerce Glossary and Acronym List*, http://www.maine.gov/ec/eaireview/eaiglossary.htm

10. *Web Services Federation Language (WS-Federation) (Version 1.0, 8 July 2003),* *http://specs.xmlsoap.org/ws/2003/07/secext/WS-Federation.pdf*

11. whatis.com, *http://whatis.techtarget.com*

12. Department of Homeland Security: *Security in the Software Lifecycle: Making Software Development Processes—and Software Produced by Them—More Secure Version 1.0,* *https://buildsecurityin.us-cert.gov*

13. *IETF RFC 2818 HTTP over TLS,* *http://www.ietf.org/rfc/rfc2818.txt*

14. *Open Grid Services Architecture Glossary of Terms (25 January 2005),* *http://www.gridforum.org/documents/GFD.44.pdf*

15. Irani, Romin, *Web Services Intermediaries: Adding Value to Web Services (21 November 2001),* *http://www.Webservicesarchitect.com/*

16. *IETF RFC 1501: The Kerberos Network Authentication Service,* *http://www.ietf.org/rfc/rfc1510.txt*

17. *OASIS XACML 2.0 Specification,* *http://docs.oasis-open.org/xacml/2.0/access_control-xacml-2.0-core-spec-os.pdf*

18. NIST SP 800-32, *Introduction to Public Key Technology and the Federal PKI Infrastructure,* February 26, 2001, *http://csrc.nist.gov/publications/nistpubs/800-32/sp800-32.pdf*

19. *W3C Glossary and Dictionary,* *http://www.w3.org/2003/glossary*

20. *Meta Access Management System Federated Identity and Access Mgmt Glossary,* *https://mams.melcoe.mq.edu.au/zope/mams/kb/glossary/view*

21. OASIS: *A Brief Introduction to XACML (14 March 2003),* *http://www.oasis-open.org/committees/download.php/2713/Brief_Introduction_to_XACML.html*

22. *Web Services Architecture - W3C Working Group Note 11 February 2004,* *http://www.w3.org/TR/2004/NOTE-ws-arch-20040211*

23. *Department of Defense (DoD) Information Assurance (IA) and Computer Network Defense (CND) Strategies: A Comprehensive Review of Common Needs and Capability Gaps State-of-the-Art Report (SOAR) (21 July 2005 - TAT-06284),* *http://iac.dtic.mil/iatac/reports.html* (accessible from .mil and .gov domains only)

24. *OASIS XACML Profile for Role Based Access Control (RBAC) (Committee Draft 01, 13 February 2004),* *http://docs.oasis-open.org/xacml/cd-xacml-rbac-profile-01.pdf*

25. *Glossary for the OASIS Security Assertion Markup Language (SAML) V2.0,* *http://www.oasis-open.org/committees/download.php/11886/saml-glossary-2.0-os.pdf*

26. NIST ITL Bulletin, *Security Implications of Active Content,* March 2000, *http://csrc.nist.gov/publications/nistbul/03-00.pdf*

27. *SSL 3.0 specification,* *http://wp.netscape.com/eng/ssl3)*

28. *IETF RFC 2246: The TLS Protocol,* *http://www.ietf.org/rfc/rfc2246.txt?number=2246*

29. *Apache Portals Project home page,* *http://portals.apache.org*

30. *Web Services Interoperability Organization (WS-I) Basic Profile Version 1.1 (10 April 2006),* *http://www.ws-i.org/Profiles/BasicProfile-1.1.html*

31. *IBM Web Services Security (WS-Security) Version 1.1 (5 April 2002),* *http://www.oasis-open.org/committees/download.php/16790/wss-v1.1-spec-os-SOAPMessageSecurity.pdf*

32. *Web Services Description Language (WSDL) 1.1,* *http://www.w3.org/TR/wsdl*

33. *World Wide Web Consortium (W3C) XML Encryption Syntax and Processing,* *http://www.w3.org/TR/xmlenc-core*

34. Intelligence Community Metatdata Working Group Information Security Marking v2.0.2 Downloads page, *https://www.icmwg.org/ic_security/index.asp*

35. World Wide Web Consortium (W3C): *Extensible Markup Language (XML)* , *http://www.w3.org/XML*

Appendix D—Acronyms and Abbreviations

Acronyms and abbreviations used in the *Guide to Securing Web Services* are listed below.

AA Attribute Authority
ABAC Attribute Based Access Control
ACL Access Control List
AD Active Directory
AES Advanced Encryption Standard
API Application Programming Interface

B2B Business-To-Business
BPML Business Process Markup Language
BPSS Business Process Specification Schema

CA Certificate Authority
CAPCO Controlled Access Program Coordination Office
CGI Common Gateway Interface
CLR Common Language Runtime
COM Component Object Model
CORBA Common Object Request Broker Architecture
COTS Commercial Off-the-Shelf
CRL Certificate Revocation List

DAML DARPA Agent Markup Language
DAO Data Access Object
DARPA Defense Advanced Research Projects Agency
DCE Distributed Computing Environment
DDMS DoD Discovery Metadata Standard
DoD Department of Defense
DoS Denial of Service
DTD Document Type Definition

ebXML Electronic Business XML
EDI Electronic Data Interchange
EPAL Enterprise Privacy Authorization Language

FDA Food and Drug Administration
FDCE Federated Development and Certification Environment
FIPS Federal Information Processing Standard
FISMA Federal Information Security Management Act

GIG Global Information Grid
GOTS Government Off-the-Shelf
GUI Graphical User Interface

HIPAA Health Insurance Portability and Accountability Act
HL7 Health Level 7
HSPD Homeland Security Presidential Directive
HTML HyperText Markup Language
HTTP HyperText Transfer Protocol

HTTPS	HyperText Transfer Protocol over SSL/TLS
I&A	Identification and Authentication
IA	Information Assurance
IC	Intelligence Community
IDS	Intrusion Detection System
IDFF	Identity Federation Framework
IDMS	Identity Management System
ID-WSF	Identity Web Services Framework
IETF	Internet Engineering Task Force
IP	Identity Provider
IPsec	Internet Protocol Security
ISM	Information Security Marketing
IT	Information Technology
ITL	Information Technology Laboratory
Java EE	Java Platform, Enterprise Edition
JAXR	Java API for XML Registries
JSM	Java Security Manager
JVM	Java Virtual Machine
LDAP	Lightweight Directory Access Protocol
MAC	Mandatory Access Control
MEP	Message Exchange Pattern
MSWG	Metadata Standards Working Group
NACI	National Agency Check and Inquiries
NCES	NetCentric Enterprise Services
NIST	National Institute of Standards and Technology
OASIS	Organization for Advancement of Structured Information Standards
OCSP	Online Certificate Status Protocol
OGSA	Open Grid Services Architecture
OMB	Office of Management and Budget
OSS	Open Source Software
OWL-S	Web Ontology Language for Web Services
PAC	Privilege Attribute Certificate
PAOS	Reverse SOAP
PBAC	Policy Based Access Control
PDP	Policy Decision Point
PEP	Policy Enforcement Point
PII	Personally Identifiable Information
PKI	Public Key Infrastructure
QoP	Quality of Protection
QoS	Quality of Service
RAdAC	Risk Adaptive (Adaptable) Access Control
RBAC	Role Based Access Control

RDBMS	Relational DataBase Management System
REST	Representational State Transfer
SAML	Security Assertion Markup Language
SMTP	Simple Mail Transport Protocol
SOA	Service Oriented Architecture
SP	Special Publication
SPL	Structured Product Labeling
SQL	Structured Query Language
SSL	Secure Sockets Layer
SSO	Single Sign On
STS	Security Token Service
SWSA	Semantic Web Services Architecture
TC	Technical Committee
TLS	Transport Layer Security
TTP	Trusted Third Party
UBR	Universal Business Registry
UDDI	Universal Description, Discovery, and Integration
UN/CEFACT	United Nations Centre for Trade Facilitation and Electronic Business
URI	Uniform Resource Identifier
URL	Uniform Resource Locator
UUID	Universally Unique Identifier
VB	Visual Basic
VB.NET	Visual Basic for .Net
VPN	Virtual Private Network
W3C	World Wide Web Consortium
WAYF	Where Are You From?
WS	Web Services
WSDL	Web Services Description Language
WS-I	Web Services Interoperability
WSS4J	Web Services Security for Java
XACML	eXtensible Access Control Markup Language
XKMS	XML Key Management Service
XML	eXtensible Markup Language
XrML	eXtensible Rights Markup Language
XSL	XML Style Sheet
XSLT	eXtensible Stylesheet Language Transformation

Appendix E—Print Resources

The following books may be helpful in providing the reader with a deeper understanding of the security concerns, standards, and technologies associated with Web services and service oriented architectures. Papers and other documents that are available both in print and online formats are listed in Appendix F, and are not referenced below.

E.1 Web Services and SOA: Background Information

Alonso, Gustavo, et al, *Web Services Concepts, Architectures and Applications,* Springer, 2003

Bishop, Matt, *Computer Security: Art and Science*, Pearson Education, 2003

Dick, Kevin, *XML: A Manager's Guide*, Addison Wesley Professional, 2002

Erl, Thomas, *Service-Oriented Architecture (SOA): Concepts, Technology, and Design*, Prentice Hall PTR, 2005

Erl, Thomas, *Service-Oriented Architecture: A Field Guide to Integrating XML and Web Services*, Prentice Hall PTR, 2004

Huang, Y., Kintala, C., Kolettis, N., and Fulton, N. D.: Software Rejuvenation: Analysis, Module and Applications (Proceedings of the 25th Symposium on Fault Tolerant Computing, June 1995) (IEEE 1995)

Kaye, Doug, *Loosely Coupled—The Missing Pieces of Web Services*, RDS Press, 2003

Manes, Anne Thomas, *Web Services: A Manager's Guide*, Addison Wesley Professional, 2003

Newcomer, Eric and Lomow, Greg, *Understanding SOA with Web Services*, Addison Wesley Professional, 2004

Potts, Stephen and Kopak, Mike, *Teach Yourself Web Services in 24 Hours*, Sams, 2003

Stanek, William R., *XML Pocket Consultant*, Microsoft Press, 2002

Zimmerman, Olaf, et al, *Perspectives on Web Services: Applying SOAP, WSDL and UDDI to Real-World Projects*, Springer Professional Computing, 2005

E.2 Web Services Security

Andrews, Mike and Whittaker, James A., *How to Break Web Software: Functional and Security Testing of Web Applications and Web Services*, Addison-Wesley Professional, 2006

Douranee, Blake, *XML Security*, McGraw-Hill Osborne Media, 2002

Hartman, Bret, et al, *Mastering Web Services Security*, Wiley Publishing, Inc., 2003

Hollar, Rickland and Murphy, Richard, *Enterprise Web Services Security*, Charles River Media/Thomson, 2005

Janakiraman, Murali, et al, *Professional Web Services Security*, Wrox Press Ltd., 2002

Niles, Donald E., III and Niles, Kitty, *Secure XML: The New Syntax for Signatures and Encryption,* Addison-Wesley, 2002

O'Neill, Mark, et al, *Web Services Security*, McGraw-Hill Osborne Media, 2003

Proceedings of the ACM 2004 Workshop on Secure Web Service, SWS '04, ACM, 2004

Proceedings of the ACM 2005 Workshop on Secure Web Service, SWS '05, ACM, 2005

Rosenberg, Jothy and Remy, David, *Securing Web Services with WS-Security: Demystifying WS-Security, WS-Policy, SAML, XML Signature, and XML Encryption,* Sams, 2004

Viega, John and McGraw, Gary, *Building Secure Software*, Addison Wesley, 2001

Wiehler, Gerhard, *Mobility, Security and Web Services: Technologies and Service-Oriented Architectures for a New Era of IT Solutions*, Wiley-VCH/Siemens, 2004

Appendix F—Online Resources

The following online resources may be helpful in providing the reader with a deeper understanding of the security concerns, standards, and technologies associated with Web services and service-oriented architectures.

F.1 Web Services Overviews and Tutorials

Resource	URL
California Enterprise Architecture Program: Service Oriented Architecture (September 2006)	http://www.cio.ca.gov/calT/pdf/SOA_Security_White_Paper.pdf
Frank P. Coyle: "XML, Web Services, and the Changing Face of Distributed Computing" (ACM Ubiquity)	http://www.acm.org/ubiquity/views/f_coyle_1.html
Hamid Nezhad, et al: Securing Service-Based Interactions : Issues and Directions (April 2005)	http://dsonline.computer.org/WAS/
Jason Bloomberg: "Principles of SOA" (Application Development Trends, 28 February 2003)	http://www.adtmag.com/article.aspx?id=7345
Jay Unger and Matt Haynos, IBM: "A visual tour of Open Grid Services Architecture"	http://www.ibm.com/developerworks/grid/library/gr-visual/
Joseph Chiusano, Booz Allen Hamilton: "The Current and Emerging State of Web Services Standards" (Quarterly Emerging Technology Components Conference, March 2004)	http://web-services.gov/Chiusano32304.ppt
Liberty ID-WSF Overview v1.1	http://www.projectliberty.org/liberty/content/download/1307/8286/file/liberty-idwsf-overview-v1.1.pdf
Luis Felipe Cabrera, et al, Microsoft Corp.: An Introduction to the Web Services Architecture and Its Specifications (Version 2.0, Oct. 2004)	http://msdn2.microsoft.com/en-us/library/ms996441.aspx
OASIS SAML Technical Overview	http://www.oasis-open.org/committees/download.php/20645/sstc-saml-tech-overview-2%200-draft-10.pdf
OASIS Using WSDL in a UDDI Registry	http://www.oasis-open.org/committees/uddi-spec/doc/tn/uddi-spec-tc-tn-wsdl-v202-20040631.htm
Scott Mitchell: An Extensive Examination of Web Services	http://aspnet.4guysfromrolla.com/articles/100803-1.aspx
Tony Baer, Ron Schmelzer: "The Elements of Web Services" (Application Development Trends, 2 December 2002)	http://www.adtmag.com/article.aspx?id=7024
Venu Vasudevan: "A Web Services Primer" (O'Reilly webservices.xml.com, 4 April 2001)	http://webservices.xml.com/pub/a/ws/2001/04/04/webservices/index.html
W3C WS-Policy Primer	http://www.w3.org/TR/ws-policy-primer/

F.2 Web Services Security Standards

Standard	URL
Current Web Service Security Standards	
Defense Discovery Metadata Standard (DDMS)	http://www.afei.org/news/ddms.pdf
IBM, Microsoft, BEA, et al: Web Services Security Policy Language (WS-SecurityPolicy)	http://specs.xmlsoap.org/ws/2005/07/securitypolicy/ws-securitypolicy.pdf

Standard	URL
IBM, Microsoft, BEA, et al: WS-Policy	http://specs.xmlsoap.org/ws/2004/09/policy/ws-policy.pdf
IBM, Microsoft, BEA, et al: WS-ReliableMessaging	http://specs.xmlsoap.org/ws/2005/02/rm/ws-reliablemessaging.pdf
IETF/W3C: XML Signature	http://www.w3.org/Signature/
OASIS Web Services Reliable Exchange TC: WS-ReliableMessaging	http://www.oasis-open.org/committees/tc_home.php?wg_abbrev=ws-rx
OASIS WS-Reliability Standard	http://www.oasis-open.org/committees/tc_home.php?wg_abbrev=wsrm
OASIS XML Cover Pages: Application Vulnerability Markup Languages	http://xml.coverpages.org/appSecurity.html
OASIS: electronic business eXtensible Markup Language (ebXML)	http://www.ebxml.org/
OASIS: eXtensible Access Control Markup Language (XACML)	http://www.oasis-open.org/committees/tc_home.php?wg_abbrev=xacml
OASIS: eXtensible Access Control Markup Language (XACML), Core and Hierarchical Role Based Access Control Profile	http://docs.oasis-open.org/xacml/2.0/access_control-xacml-2.0-core-spec-os.pdf
OASIS Security Services (SAML)	http://www.oasis-open.org/committees/tc_home.php?wg_abbrev=security
OASIS Security Services (SAML), SAML Profiles	http://docs.oasis-open.org/security/saml/v2.0/saml-profiles-2.0-os.pdf
OASIS Security Services (SAML), Security and Privacy Considerations for SAML	http://docs.oasis-open.org/security/saml/v2.0/saml-sec-consider-2.0-os.pdf
OASIS Universal Description, Discovery and Integration (UDDI)	http://www.oasis-open.org/committees/uddi-spec/doc/spec/v3/uddi-v3.0.2-20041019.htm
OASIS Web Services Secure Conversation Language (WS-SecureConversation)	http://docs.oasis-open.org/ws-sx/ws-secureconversation/200512/ws-secureconversation-1.3-os.pdf
OASIS Web Services Security (WSS)	http://www.oasis-open.org/committees/tc_home.php?wg_abbrev=wss
OASIS Web Services Security (WS-Security)	http://www.oasis-open.org/committees/download.php/16790/wss-v1.1-spec-os-SOAPMessageSecurity.pdf
OASIS XML Common Biometric Format (XCBF)	http://www.oasis-open.org/committees/tc_home.php?wg_abbrev=xcbf
Semantic Web Services Architecture Requirements	http://www.daml.org/services/swsa/swsa-requirements.html
Simple eXtensible Identity Protocol (SXIP) 2.0	http://sxip.org/
UDDI.org v2 Programmer's API	http://uddi.org/pubs/ProgrammersAPI-V2.04-Published-20020719.pdf
W3C SOAP Version 1.2 Part 1	http://www.w3.org/TR/soap12-part1
W3C Web Service Policy Working Group: WS-Policy	http://www.w3.org/2002/ws/policy/
W3C XML Encryption	http://www.w3.org/Encryption/
W3C XML Key Management Specification (XKMS)	http://www.w3.org/TR/xkms/
WS-I Basic Security Profile	http://www.ws-i.org/deliverables/workinggroup.aspx?wg=basicsecurity
WS-I Security Challenges	http://www.ws-i.org/Profiles/BasicSecurity/SecurityChallenges-1.0.pdf

Standard	URL
Emerging Web Service Security Standards	
OASIS Web Services Secure Exchange (WS-SX): WS-SecureConversation, WS-SecurityPolicy, WS-Trust	http://www.oasis-open.org/committees/tc_home.php?wg_abbrev=ws-sx
OASIS: LegalXML eNotarization	http://www.oasis-open.org/committees/tc_home.php?wg_abbrev=legalxml-enotary
Trust Framework Standards	
IBM, Microsoft, BEA, et al: WS-Trust	http://specs.xmlsoap.org/ws/2005/02/trust/WS-Trust.pdf
IBM: WS-Federation	http://specs.xmlsoap.org/ws/2003/07/secext/WS-Federation.pdf
Liberty Alliance Project	http://www.projectliberty.org/
Shibboleth	http://shibboleth.internet2.edu/
Supporting Standards (Current and Emerging)	
IETF RFC 2246: Transport Layer Security (TLS) version 1.0	http://www.ietf.org/rfc/rfc2246.txt
IETF RFC 2459: X.509 Public Key Infrastructure Certificate and Certificate Revocation List (CRL) Profile	http://www.ietf.org/rfc/rfc2459.txt
IETF RFC 2818: HyperText Transfer Protocol (HTTP) over TLS (HTTPS)	http://www.ietf.org/rfc/rfc2818.txt
International Telecommunication Union (ITU): Recommendation X.509 - Public-key and attribute certificate frameworks	http://www.itu.int/rec/T-REC-X.509/en
Netscape: Secure Sockets Layer (SSL) 3.0 Internet Draft specification	http://wp.netscape.com/eng/ssl3/ssl-toc.html
OASIS Digital Signature Services (DSS)	http://www.oasis-open.org/committees/tc_home.php?wg_abbrev=dss
OASIS Provisioning Services	http://www.oasis-open.org/committees/tc_home.php?wg_abbrev=provision
OASIS Public Key Infrastructure (PKI)	http://www.oasis-open.org/committees/tc_home.php?wg_abbrev=pki

F.3 U.S. Government Publications

Standard	URL
FIPS 140-2, *Security Requirements for Cryptographic Modules*	http://csrc.nist.gov/publications/fips/fips140-2/fips1402.pdf
FIPS 186-2, *Digital Signature Standard*	http://csrc.nist.gov/publications/fips/fips186-2/fips186-2-change1.pdf
FIPS 196, *Entity Authentication Using Public Key Cryptography*	http://csrc.nist.gov/publications/fips/fips196/fips196.pdf
FIPS 201-1, *Personal Integrity Verification of Federal Employees and Contractors*	http://csrc.nist.gov/publications/fips/fips201-1/FIPS-201-1-chng1.pdf
HSPD-12, *Policy for a Common Identification Standard for Federal Employees and Contractors*	http://www.whitehouse.gov/news/releases/2004/08/20040827-8.html
IR 7298, *Glossary of Key Information Security Terms*	http://csrc.nist.gov/publications/nistir/NISTIR-7298_Glossary_Key_Infor_Security_Terms.pdf

Standard	URL
SP 800-21-1, *Guideline for Implementing Cryptography in the Federal Government*	http://csrc.nist.gov/publications/nistpubs/800-21-1/sp800-21-1_Dec2005.pdf
SP 800-25, *Federal Agency Use of Public Key Technology for Digital Signatures and Authentication*	http://csrc.nist.gov/publications/nistpubs/800-25/sp800-25.pdf
SP 800-32, *Introduction to Public Key Technology and the Federal PKI Infrastructure*	http://csrc.nist.gov/publications/nistpubs/800-32/sp800-32.pdf
SP 800-44, *Guidelines on Securing Public Web Servers*	http://csrc.nist.gov/publications/nistpubs/800-44/sp800-44.pdf
SP 800-57, *Special Publication on Key Management*	http://csrc.nist.gov/publications/nistpubs/800-57/SP800-57-Part1.pdf
SP 800-92, *Guide to Computer Security Log Management*	http://csrc.nist.gov/publications/nistpubs/800-92/SP800-92.pdf
SP 800-100, *Information Security Handbook: A Guide for Managers*	http://csrc.nist.gov/publications/nistpubs/800-100/SP800-100-Mar07-2007.pdf

F.4 Organizations

Organization	URL
Standards Bodies	
IEEE Computer Society Technical Committee on Services Computing	http://tab.computer.org/tcsc/
Internet Engineering Task Force (IETF)	http://www.ietf.org/
Java Community Process (JCP)	http://www.jcp.org/
Organization for the Advancement of Structured Information Standards (OASIS)	http://www.oasis-open.org
Web Service-Interoperability Organization (WS-I)	http://www.ws-i.org/
World Wide Web Consortium (W3C)	http://www.w3.org
Technical Initiatives	
Eclipse	http://www.eclipse.org/
The Globus Alliance	http://www.globus.org/
Consortia and Associations	
Open Web Application Security Project (OWASP)	http://www.owasp.org/index.jsp
Web Application Security Consortium	http://www.webappsec.org/

F.5 Web Pages, Sites, and Portals

Resource Name	URL
Defense Online Portal to the Global Information Grid: NCES Security Service	http://ges.dod.mil/ServiceSecurity.htm
DoD Net-Centric Enterprise Services: Core Information Assurance/Security Services	http://www.disa.mil/nces/core_enterprise_services/security_content.html
IBM developerWorks: SOA and Web services/security	http://www-128.ibm.com/developerworks/search/searchResults.jsp?searchType=1&searchSite=dW&searchScope=webservZ&query=security&Search.x=41&Search.y=14&Search=Search
Microsoft Developer Network (MSDN): Building Secure Web Services	http://msdn2.microsoft.com/en-us/webservices/Aa740661.aspx
NIST RBAC Web Site	http://csrc.nist.gov/rbac

Resource Name	URL
Sun Developer Network (SDN): Secure Java Web Services	http://java.sun.com/webservices/index.jsp
XML.org: Focus Area on Security	http://security.xml.org/

F.6 Online Forums

Forum	URL
XML Web Services Security Forum	http://www.xwss.org/

F.7 Conferences and Workshops

Event	URL
IEEE International Conference on Web Services *[note tutorial on Web services security]*	http://conferences.computer.org/icws/
IEEE Workshop on Web Services Security Oakland, CA, May 21, 2006	http://www.ieee-security.org/TC/SP2006/oakland06.html
International World Wide Web Conference Committee	http://www.iw3c2.org/
Unatek Web Services Security Conference (WSSC)	http://unatekconference.com/
Web Services Protocol Workshops (WS-Workshops)	http://msdn2.microsoft.com/en-us/webservices/aa740612.aspx
Workshop on Secure Web Services (SWS) at ACM Conference on Computer and Communications Security (CCS)	http://www.acm.org/sigs/sigsac/ccs/CCS2006/workshop.html

F.8 Online Documents

Some of these documents may also be available in hardcopy format. They are listed here rather than in Appendix E because they can be readily obtained online.

Document Reference	URL
Conference Papers	
Alex Stamos, iSEC Partners LLC: "Attacking Web Services" (OWASP AppSec DC, October 2005)	https://www.isecpartners.com/documents/iSEC-Attacking-Web-Services.OWASP.pdf
Audun Jøsang, Distributed Systems Technology Centre, et al.: "Trust requirements in Identity Management" (*Proceedings of the 2005 Australasian workshop on Grid computing and e-research*, January 2005)	http://portal.acm.org/citation.cfm?id=1082290.1082305
B. Carminati and E. Ferrari, University of Insubria at Como (Italy), and P.C.K. Hung, University of Ontario (Canada) Institute of Technology: "Web Service Composition: A Security Perspective" (*Proceedings of the 2005 International Workshop on Challenges in Web Information Retrieval and Integration [WIRI'05]*)	*To purchase from IEEE Computer Society:* http://doi.ieeecomputersociety.org/10.1109/WIRI.2005.36
Eric Yuan and Jin Tong, Booz Allen Hamilton: "Attribute-Based Access Control (ABAC) for Web Services" (*Proceedings of the New Challenges for Access Control Workshop,* April 2005)	http://lotos.csi.uottawa.ca/ncac05/yuan_18500229.ppt

Document Reference	URL
Hamid R. Motahari Nezhad, et al: "Securing Service-Based Interactions: Issues and Directions" (*IEEE Distributed Systems Online,* April 2005)	http://dsonline.computer.org/portal/site/dsonline/index.jsp?pageID=dso_level1&path=dsonline/topics/was/papers&file=motahari.xml&xsl=article.xsl
Ken Birman, Cornell University: "The Untrustworthy Web Services Revolution" (*IEEE Computer,* Feb. 2006)	*To purchase from IEEE Computer Society:* http://doi.ieeecomputersociety.org/10.1109/MC.2006.73
Marek Hatala, et al, Simon Fraser University (Surrey, BC, Canada): "Federated Security: Lightweight Security Infrastructure for Object Repositories and Web Services" (*Proceedings of the 2005 International Conference on Next Generation Web Services Practices*, 2005 [NWeSP'05])	http://www.sfu.ca/~mhatala/pubs/nwesp2005-federated-security.pdf
Neal Leavitt: "Are Web Services Finally Ready to Deliver?" (*IEEE Computer,* Nov. 2004)	*To purchase from IEEE Computer Society:* http://doi.ieeecomputersociety.org/10.1109/MC.2004.199
Takeshi Imamura, Michiaki Tatsubori, and Yuichi Nakamura, IBM/Tokyo Research Lab., and Christopher Giblin, IBM/Zurich Research Lab.: "Web Services Security Configuration in a Service-Oriented Architecture" (*Proceedings of WWW 2005*)	http://www2005.org/cdrom/docs/p1120.pdf
Academic Theses	
Thomas Schepers, University of Tilburg (Netherlands): *A View on Web Service Security: Can Current Security Standards Adequately Secure Web Services?* (Final Thesis)	http://arno.uvt.nl/show.cgi?fid=28992
Other Academic Papers and Research Reports	
D. Harrison McKnight and Norman L. Chervany, University of Minnesota: "The Meanings of Trust"	http://misrc.umn.edu/wpaper/WorkingPapers/9604.pdf
E. Kleiner and A.W. Roscoe, Oxford University: "On the Relationship between Web Services Security and Traditional Protocols" (May 2005)	http://web.comlab.ox.ac.uk/oucl/work/bill.roscoe/publications/104.pdf
Jess Thompson, et al, The Gartner Group: "Security Pattern Standards Face a Long Road to Maturity" (October 2003)	*To purchase from Gartner Group:* http://www.gartner.com/DisplayDocument?doc_cd=118238
Jun Han, Swinburne University of Technology (Hawthorn, VIC, Australia): "A Software Engineering Perspective for Services Security" (July 2004)	http://www.it.swin.edu.au/personal/jhan/jhanPapers/gcc04.pdf
Matthew Schwartz, IT Compliance Institute: "State of the Union: Interoperability between SOA Security Standards" (10 May 2005)	http://www.itcinstitute.org/display.aspx?id=295
Pete Lindstrom, Spire Security LLC: "Attacking and Defending Web Services: A Research Report" (Jan. 2004)	http://forumsystems.com/papers/Attacking_and_Defending_WS.pdf
Ray Wagner, The Gartner Group: "Making Sense of Web Services Security Standards" (August 2003)	*To purchase from Gartner Group:* http://www.gartner.com/DisplayDocument?doc_cd=116961
Ray Wagner, The Gartner Group: "Web Services Security Standards Aren't Enough" (July 2003)	*To purchase from Gartner Group:* http://www.gartner.com/DisplayDocument?doc_cd=116362
Rafae Bhatti, et al: "Access Control in Dynamic XML-based Web-Services with X-RBAC"	http://www.rafaebhatti.com/academics/research/papers/ICWS_2003.pdf
Yaron Goland: "SOA Security - Authentication" (2 Nov. 2005)	http://www.goland.org/soasecurityauthentication
Yaron Goland: "SOA Security - Encryption" (9 Nov. 2005)	http://www.goland.org/soaencryption
Yaron Goland: "SOA Security - The Myth of Non-Repudiation" (8 Nov. 2005)	http://www.goland.org/soanonrepudiation

Document Reference	URL
Government Papers	
Defense Information Systems Agency (DISA): *A Security Architecture for Net-Centric Enterprise Services (NCES)* (Version 0.3 Pilot - 1 March 2004)	http://www.estrategy.gov/documents/disa0304.pdf http://horizontalfusion.dtic.mil/docs/specs/20040310_NCES_Security_Arc.pdf
Web Services Security Issues in a Justice Environment	http://it.ojp.gov/documents/asp/security_topics/section1.htm
Vendor Papers	
IBM Corporation and Microsoft Corporation: "Federation of Identities in a Web Services World" (Version 1.0, July 2003)	ftp://www6.software.ibm.com/software/developer/library/ws-fedworld.pdf http://people.cs.vt.edu/~kafura/cs6204/Readings/Authentication/FederationOfIdentities-WhitePaper.pdf
IBM Redbooks Paper: "Federated Identity Management and Secure Web Services" (August 2003)	http://www.redbooks.ibm.com/redpapers/pdfs/redp3678.pdf
Kim Cameron, Microsoft Corporation: "The Laws of Identity" (May 2005)	http://www.identityblog.com/stories/2004/12/09/thelaws.html
Articles from the Technology Press	
J. Epstein, G. McGraw and S. Matsumoto, Cigital Inc.: "Software Security and SOA: Danger, Will Robinson!" (*IEEE Security & Privacy*, Jan./Feb. 2006)	http://www.cigital.com/papers/download/bsi12-soa.doc.pdf
Luís Iribarne, University of Almería (Spain): "Web Components: A Comparison between Web Services and Software Components" (*Revista Colombiana de Computación/Columbian Journal of Computation,* June 2004)	http://www.unab.edu.co/editorialunab/revistas/rcc/pdfs/r51_art4_c.pdf
Paul Madsen: "WS-Trust: Interoperable Security for Web Services" (O'Reilly webservices.xml.com, July 2003)	http://www.xml.com/pub/a/ws/2003/06/24/ws-trust.html
Schahram Dustdar and Wolfgang Schreiner, Vienna (Austria) University of Technology: "A Survey on Web Services Composition" (*International Journal of Web and Grid Services,* Vol. 1 No. 1, 2005)	http://www.infosys.tuwien.ac.at/Staff/sd/papers/A%20survey%20on%20web%20services%20composition_Dustdar_Schreiner_inPress.pdf
Sridhar Ravuthula, developer.com: "Fundamentals of Data Security" ("Web Services Application and Security", Part 3)	http://www.developer.com/services/article.php/2109481
Sridhar Ravuthula, developer.com: "Web Services Applications and Security", Parts 1 and 2	http://www.developer.com/services/article.php/1550461 http://www.developer.com/services/article.php/1555791
Presentations and Tutorials	
Andrew Nash, Reactivity: "xmlCoP Interoperable Trust Networks" (January 2005)	http://www.xml.gov/presentations/reactivity/trust.ppt http://www.xml.gov/presentations/reactivity/trust.htm
Andy Gordon, Microsoft Research: "Secure Global Computing with XML Web Services: Theory and Practice" (tutorial at EEF Global Computing Summer School, Edinburgh, Scotland, July 2003)	http://www.lfcs.inf.ed.ac.uk/events/global-computing/slides/gordon.PDF
Andy Gordon, Microsoft Research: "Web Service Security: Theory and Practice" (crash course for faculty and PhDs, Saint John's College, Cambridge Univ., March 2003)	http://www.gosecure.ca/SecInfo/library/WebApplication/webservicesec.ppt

Document Reference	URL
Christopher J. "Kit" Lueder, MITRE Corporation: "XML Security Threat Analysis" (January 2002)	http://xml.gov/presentations/mitre4/index.html http://xml.gov/presentations/mitre4/XMLsecurity.ppt
Mike Edwards and Hedley Proctor, IBM (Hursley Park, UK): "Web Services Security - Theory and Practice"	http://www.websphereusergroup.org.uk/downloads/04oct/Web%20Services%20Security_06102004.pdf
Steve Orrin, Intel Corporation/ Sarvega Inc.: "Securing Enterprise/ Government SOA & Web Services Applications: The Lifecycle & Threat Perspectives" (tutorial, Annual Computer Security Applications Conference [ACSAC] 2005)	*To request a copy, send email request to:* steve.orrin@intel.com

F.9 Web Service Security Implementations

Resource	URL
Open Source Standards Implementations	
Apache WSS implementation for Java (WSS4J)	http://ws.apache.org/wss4j
Apache XML Security implementation	http://xml.apache.org/security
Open source WS-Security implementation for Apache Axis	http://axis-wsse.sourceforge.net
OpenSAML 1.1 - Open Source Security Assertion Markup Language implementation	http://www.opensaml.org
Project X-Access: X-RBACv1.0 and X-GTRBACv1.1 and v1.2 implementations	http://shay.ecn.purdue.edu/~iisrl/x-access.htm
Sun Microsystems open source XACML 2.0 Implementation	http://sunxacml.sourceforge.net
Web Services Summit (August 2004) Panel on Web Services Security Issues: Video and MP3 Audio (Podcast) Programs	http://www.webservicessummit.com/SDSIC_Aug2004.htm
Open Source Trust Framework Implementations	
Apache Shibboleth implementation	http://shibboleth.internet2.edu/
PERSEUS Project (Portal-Enabled Resources via Shibbolized End-User Security) *[R&D]*	http://www.angel.ac.uk/PERSEUS
Shibboleth-aware Portals and Information Environments Project (SPIE) *[R&D]*	http://www.oucs.ox.ac.uk/rts/spie

F.10 Other Developer Resources

Resource	URL
Apache Trust Service Integration Kit (TSIK) (formerly Verisign TSIK)	http://incubator.apache.org/tsik
DHS Build Security In Portal	https://buildsecurityin.us-cert.gov
Microsoft Research, Cambridge (UK): Samoa: Formal Tools for Securing Web Services *[R&D]*	http://research.microsoft.com/projects/Samoa
NIST SAMATE Project	http://samate.nist.gov
Sun Microsystems: Java Web Services Developer Pack 1.6 TUTORIAL - Chapter 4: Introduction to XML and Web Services Security	http://java.sun.com/webservices/docs/1.6/tutorial/doc/XWS-SecurityIntro.html#wp540763

www.ingramcontent.com/pod-product-compliance
Lightning Source LLC
Chambersburg PA
CBHW080427060326
40689CB00019B/4404

* 9 7 8 1 4 7 5 0 2 3 7 9 4 *